"This book presents a compelling new integrated leadership model that defines behaviors for successful execution in the face of a fast-paced, ever-changing environment. The authors offer clear direction for senior managers and professionals on how to improve results and achieve a motivating work environment."

—Daniel Vasella, Chairman and CEO,
Novartis International AG

"Filled with practical, real-life examples, *When Professionals Have to Lead* is essential reading for anyone managing professionals doing creative and intellectually demanding work. In many ways, the integrated leadership model presented in the book is simple, but that is its beauty. By following the authors' advice, firms will become much more strategically focused and inclusive places to work and they will see their investment pay off handsomely."

—Tom Watson, former Vice Chairman,
Omnicom Group; dean, Omnicom University

"The authors provide remarkable insights for leaders of service-oriented firms on how to address critical issues of strategy and human capital. A must-read for leaders managing diverse teams across the world."

—Naina Lal Kidwai, Group General Manager
and Country Head, HSBC India

Global professional firms are facing ever more difficult challenges. *When Professionals Have to Lead* describes a new model of professional firm leadership, developed by the authors after many years working in professional firms, which is both insightful and practical. In thinking through the competitive and organizational ramifications of operating in different markets, or ensuring the alignment of a firm's strategy, organization, and talent, the authors provide ideas and examples that will help all professionals become effective leaders."

—Thierry Porté, President and CEO, Shinsei Bank, Ltd.

When Professionals
Have to Lead

When Professionals Have to Lead

A NEW MODEL FOR HIGH

PERFORMANCE

Thomas J. DeLong

John J. Gabarro

Robert J. Lees

HARVARD BUSINESS SCHOOL PRESS

Boston, Massachusetts

Printed in the United States of America
11 10 09 08 07   5 4 3 2 1

Library of Congress Cataloging-in-Publication Data

DeLong, Thomas.
  When professionals have to lead : a new model for high performance /
Thomas J. DeLong, John J. Gabarro, Robert J. Lees.
    p. cm.
  ISBN-13: 978-1-4221-1737-8 (hardcover : alk. paper)
  ISBN-10: 1-4221-1737-5
1. Professional corporations—Management. 2. Leadership. 3. Professions
—Recruiting. I. Gabarro, John J. II. Lees, Robert J., 1948- III. Title.
  HD62.65.D45 2007
  658.4'092—dc22

                                                              2007023057

The paper used in this publication meets the requirements of the American National Standard for Permanence of Paper for Publications and Documents in Libraries and Archives Z39.48-1992.

To Jay W. Lorsch

Friend, colleague, and teacher

A pioneer for having recognized
that professional service firms
were a breed apart

Contents

     Motivating, Retaining, and Developing Your Talent

8   The Essential B Player   171
     The Heart and Soul of an Organization

9   The Challenge of Connection   187
     Connecting the Firm to the Future

     Notes   *209*
     Index   *213*
     About the Authors   *231*

Acknowledgments

As ever, the material in the book is the result of many conversations with a wide range of people. The professionals we have taught over the past twenty years at Harvard Business School and during in-company programs around the world have taken the time to debate our ideas and have contributed to our thinking. Their patience with our questioning and ongoing inquiry assisted us immeasurably in developing the insights that form the core of this book.

We must recognize the contribution our colleagues have made. Their names may not be on the cover, but they will recognize their contributions as they turn the pages. In particular, we would like to thank our colleague Jay Lorsch. Jay, Jack, and their colleagues established Harvard's Leading Professional Service Firms Program in 1995, and that program's success and its role as a catalyst in developing our thinking is primarily due to Jay's continued passion and thirst for understanding professional firms. We have also benefited greatly from the deep support and keen criticism of a wonderful group of colleagues in the Organizational Behavior unit at the Harvard Business School, especially Bower Fellow Michael Beer, John Barron, Linda Hill, Rakesh Khurana, Boris Groysberg, Paul Lawrence, and David Thomas. Nitin Nohria, a constant supporter, has helped shape the book in innumerable ways. So too has Ashish Nanda, providing us with helpful feedback. In particular, we thank Emily Heaphy, whose research assistance helped ground the book and who wrote a first draft of chapter 5, and Mike Yoshino, who had to withdraw as a coauthor early in the project but whose contributions to chapter 6 have made a substantial difference.

In addition to these stalwart friends, a great number of colleagues gave us invaluable criticism and suggestions on the first draft, which have profoundly affected the book's eventual form. Topmost on this list is Carl Sloane, who brought not only his deep insights as an academic, but also his deep understanding of the phenomena as a founder of Temple, Barker, Sloane and as founding CEO of Mercer Consulting. Our thoughts and ideas have been improved by Paul McKinnon, Mike Mister, Des Woods, Liz Baltesz, John Lucy, and Derek Klyhn, who have all challenged our thinking. Their contributions have helped us enormously, as did Andrew Collins's. Andrew died of cancer in 2002, but his thoughtful and penetrative contributions have stayed with us.

We have used many real-life examples of truly excellent professional firms throughout the book, and our thanks go to the people who gave their time and shared their insights with us. We would like to thank the real estate team at Herbert Smith for their openness and honesty. We also benefited greatly from the feedback of three leaders of major professional service firms: Peter Cornell, managing partner of Clifford Chance; John Haley, CEO of Watson Wyatt; and Paul Osling, Global COO of Ernst & Young, who gave us penetrating and useful criticisms that forced us to make sharper and clearer distinctions.

It is impossible to discuss the publishing of any book without reference to the many people involved in the process. Major thanks go to our assistants Emily Hall and Amie Evans for helping to put the manuscript together and for their patience in responding to our many requests for help. We don't know how they did it, but we will be eternally grateful. Our book is demonstrably better because of Kirsten Sandberg's insistence that we reframe our material around our integrated leadership model. The book is also much improved by the editors at the Press, including Jane Gebhart, whose ability to make simple changes that enhance the clarity of our writing cannot be understated. We are also greatly indebted to Bruce Wexler. Bruce was our constant companion during the writing of the book, and his help in editing our occasionally incoherent thoughts and in creating a single voice, demand special thanks.

Thanks finally to Vineeta, Marilyn, and Daphne for providing love, support, and candid feedback in all areas of our lives.

Introduction

The nature of professional services is changing, as firms experience greater internal demands from their professionals and greater external demands from clients. Associates have development needs that often aren't being met; clients expect firms to be all things to all people, requesting help in areas where firms may have little or no expertise. In this environment, senior partners, practice group heads, and other leaders of professional service firms, or PSFs, require guidance about how to lead and manage within such a changing world.

Unfortunately, the majority of leaders are using old frameworks and ways of thinking to fashion makeshift behaviors to meet these new challenges. For many, the answer is to work longer hours and become exhausted. Or they assume that traveling more than in the past will enable them to get problems under control. Or as the market changes, they focus more of their energies on differentiation in the marketplace. Or they keep hiring the best and the brightest, assuming that this investment in talent will pay off in the long-term viability of their human capital.

We have written this book for leaders who see the need for changing the way they lead and manage professional service firms but who lack a framework for doing so. We introduce what we call an *integrated leadership model*, which is designed to stimulate thinking and facilitate the changes that high-performing firm leaders want to enact. As you will discover, this new model is applicable whether you are in charge of a large firm or are a partner managing a small group of professionals or directing the energies of the firm on smaller projects. You can use this framework to help transform your group or organization or to make minor changes in your firm without impacting strategy and direction. It offers ideas about how to set a new direction and how to gain greater commitment to that direction at all levels of the firm. It also suggests ways to enhance execution of that new direction. And it provides insights about how the personal examples of firm leaders can have an enormously positive impact on direction, commitment, and execution.

In writing this book, we were fully aware that professional service firms are both the most challenging and the most exciting type of organization to lead. When you put an amalgam of very smart professionals together to work on significant client problems, you have the potential for creating an endlessly exciting culture of highly committed professionals. At the same time, you run the risk of creating an organization characterized by frustration, unmet needs, lack of shared purpose, poor morale, and, ultimately, bad work.

Today, professional service firm leaders increasingly want to avoid the latter and do whatever is necessary to achieve the former. They recognize that they need help in understanding why they must lead more effectively, and they are open to ideas about how to do so. At long last they accept that they cannot assume human capital issues will take care of themselves and just disappear. Leaders of professional service firms realize that through conscientious effort, changes can be made that impact the top and bottom lines of their firms.

We wrote this book because leaders in professional service firms have asked for a guide, for new underpinnings and frameworks to help steer their thinking. Leaders at all levels are trying to figure out how to keep the right professionals from leaving the organization at the wrong time. They worry that young associates are not remaining in the professions, while associates report that their career expectations are not being met through the various stages of their careers. Partners are also frustrated not only with uncommitted professionals but with the dynamics and economics of their firms.

Firms are growing larger. Leaders want to keep a familylike culture, but it is difficult to maintain this culture in an intensively competitive, growth-oriented, time-deficient environment. Managing partners ask their partners in professional service firms not only to bring in and develop new business but to do more managing. Although such leaders went into their professions to be technical experts and problem solvers, they spend a great deal of time dealing with human capital issues.[1] This creates frustrations for leaders who must spend more time in activities like coaching and mentoring that keep them from their "real" work. Few entered their professions to become managers, yet they now lead practices, offices, and even their firms. They are unclear about how to deal with this dilemma. We will address this and other dilemmas and suggest appropriate solutions.

We also wrote this book for leaders in professional service firms who like their work but feel overloaded and conflicted most of the time. No matter what these leaders are doing, they think they should be doing something else. They want to do something about associates who leave prematurely or partners who feel disenfranchised or ignored, but they lack the time and energy. While internal pressures mount, the managing partner worries about whether the firm should merge or take on work that doesn't exactly fit the niche of what the firm does. Simultaneously, senior partners realize that they have not created a succession planning process throughout the organization; there are too many individuals on the list for promotion to partner, and senior partners worry about the economic implications for the firm if all are promoted.

The good news is that we have observed and worked with professional service firms that get large pieces of the puzzle right. We see organizations that are actively engaged in transforming themselves in small and significant ways to create better places to work and better economic results. The integrated leadership model is based in large part on these observations.

We offer this model to firms that don't want to repeat the sins of the past. In some firms, leaders were afraid to make any changes even though they were losing ground with competitors on a daily basis. They were doing the wrong things. They effectively neglected their associates by not having honest career development conversations. They had perfected a misguided approach to performance appraisals and processes, such as ignoring the abusive behaviors of a few of their rainmakers because they couldn't give up those economic benefits. The leaders of these organizations were expert at writing superb mission statements that professionals within the firms scoffed at.

We know that professionals who self-select into professional service firms are very skilled in their fields of expertise but are not necessarily aware of organizational dynamics, organizational practices that create aligned organizations, or the individual motivations of other professionals. Though they offer opinions on a wide range of organizational topics, these opinions may be based on erroneous assumptions. We wrote this book to help smart people make better decisions in how they manage themselves and their firms.

What We Hope You'll Learn

In chapter 2, we'll describe our leadership model and how it evolved out of the problems and opportunities that have bedeviled heads of firms in recent years. We'll explain why an integrated framework is much more relevant today than a "bifurcated" one in dealing with the complex, paradoxical problems firms routinely encounter.

Our third chapter addresses an issue that is central to any discussion of PSF leadership: the difference between professional service firms and their corporate brethren. The lines between service firms and product-based organizations have blurred in recent years, due in no small part to firms creating products and the corporate trend to make professional services part of their marketing mix. The integrated model maintains that many significant differences still exist, and that leaders must keep these differences in mind as they practice the four key leadership behaviors: setting direction, getting commitment to that direction, executing the direction, and setting a great personal example as a leader.

Two of the biggest issues that leaders of PSFs are wrestling with are product intensity and practice segmentation. Not long ago, products such as customized leadership programs or software programs were a nonissue for many firms and the three traditional segments of procedural firms, gray-haired firms, and rocket scientist firms dominated. Now, leaders must find the right balance between product and practice intensity. They must also address the new practice segments that have emerged, such as commoditization. We'll look at both these challenges in chapters 4 and 5. We'll also focus on how the integrated model helps firm heads deal effectively with these issues.

Chapters 6 and 7 address strategy and developing a firm's professionals, and though these topics have been the subject of other articles and books, we look at them through the lens of our model. The integration theme surfaces as we see how crucial is it to align business, talent, and the organization; we'll see how the best PSF leaders are strategic in the holistic sense of the word—they don't just issue strategic directives, they gain commitment for a new direction and take responsibility for achieving it. Similarly, they apply the same integrated approach toward motivating and developing professionals who have a high need for achievement.

Chapter 8 focuses on the solid professionals who comprise most professions, whom we call B players, and their indispensable role in highly successful professional service firms. Gaining commitment from B players and helping them execute a firm's strategy are ambitious goals, but ones that can be achieved using an integrated approach.

The final chapter emphasizes the need for cultures that help firms achieve their strategy while simultaneously inspiring and motivating their talent. Now, and especially in the future, alignment will make or break firms. It is very difficult to foster cultures that facilitate alignment when leaders view themselves only as producer-managers. Integrated leadership, as we'll see, makes it easier for all the facets of a firm to reinforce each other.

Throughout these chapters, we'll draw on the experiences of professional service firms in a wide range of industries, including consulting, law, architecture, tax advice, auditing, accounting, money management, and investment banking. We'll provide examples that illustrate how PSF leadership has been defined largely in terms of client service and technical excellence, and how competitive forces have prompted some firms to reassess this tradition and embark in new leadership directions.

Though firms face complex and difficult challenges now and in the years ahead, they also are being presented with many opportunities for growth and profit. To capitalize on these opportunities and meet new challenges effectively, an evolved leadership model is crucial. We hope that our integrated leadership approach provides this model, and that it can be used to achieve every firm's goals.

In one fashion or another, the three of us have spent most of our careers working in professional service organizations, studying them, or both. Our collective and complementary interests and experiences, together with our shared excitement about professional services as a specific genre of organization, provide both the basis and motivation for writing this book. We hope that our integrated leadership model will provide a guide for leaders and partners in professional service organizations and the unique challenges they face.

—Thomas J. DeLong
   Jack Gabarro
   Rob Lees

1

From Virtual Management to Highly Demanding Clients

Why a Fresh Leadership Approach Is Mandatory

Jeff Gardner (not his real name), a new managing partner of a medium-sized, rapidly growing Seattle consulting firm, is multitasking late into the night. While he puts the final touches on a new business presentation for an early meeting in Los Angeles the next day, he is also jotting some notes for a talk he will give at the annual partners' meeting the following week. Jeff is concerned about the firm's loss of some key professionals to competitors as well as the need to reposition the firm based on emerging trends in the industry. Made up of consultants with biotech, financial services, and software clients, Jeff's firm has to respond proactively rather than reactively; he fears that the firm is becoming too "strategic" and is losing its reputation as a problem solver.

On top of everything else, Jeff is mulling over the list of candidates he has interviewed for a chief staff officer—a position he needs to fill quickly to take some of the load off his shoulders. He wants to leave the office so he can see his kids before they go to bed, but he also knows that except for the day of the partners' meeting next week, he will be on the road constantly. It is after midnight when Jeff leaves, and he still hasn't finished everything he wanted to do, but he calculates that he'll "steal" an hour of additional working time on the 7:00 a.m. flight the next morning.

When Jeff gets home late that evening, he can't sleep. His mind is still revving at high speeds even though his body is tired. He tries to get to sleep by repeating the good news to himself: he has better than expected results to report at the annual partners' meeting. Solid growth in revenues and an even better increase in profitability, and a great recruiting season and good utilization, despite the intake of new hires, are all positive outcomes that have taken place under his watch.

But Jeff also knows that there are several problems that are worse now than a year ago when he became managing partner. For one thing, the firm's growing inability to retain enough of its best midlevel professionals galls him. These are the folks who really get the firm's work done, who supervise new associates and actually manage the teams on the ground. His most recent midlevel losses include a top case manager in the biotech strategy practice as well as a fourth-year associate who surely would have been promoted to manager next year. The first was recruited by a small biotech firm, and the second was lost to a large pharmaceutical company. Although both parted on good terms for what each described as "bet-

ter opportunities," Jeff immediately identified the subtext from reading their exit interviews: they didn't know where they stood with the
firm in terms of their career prospects, and both had received little
or inadequate coaching or performance feedback.

In fact, Jeff's HR director had warned him earlier that day that
two midlevel professionals in the firm's growing financial services
practice had also complained about lack of feedback on their performance, leaving him worried that they too might be vulnerable to
job offers. Jeff is particularly concerned that both report to Dale
Miller (not his real name), the head of the financial services practice and one of the firm's stars, whom Jeff himself had mentored. A
great professional and business developer, Dale is unfortunately an
indifferent coach and a lousy people manager. Jeff has asked the
HR director to talk to Dale about his unwillingness to spend time
providing his people with constructive feedback and learning opportunities, but Jeff knows it won't do much good. Dale is not only
stubborn, he's a star. Their firm isn't any different from other consulting groups; stars can do no wrong. Though his firm gives a lot of
lip service to the notion of professional development, the reality is
that bringing in and keeping business is what counts.

Jeff isn't blaming all the firm's retention problems on Dale.
Long hours combined with often repetitive and sometimes boring
work is another cause. For years, women associates left the firm
after having children. Now, a number of men have also departed for
reasons of work-life balance. Jeff knows that the work hours and
travel have become worse in recent years, as he himself has experienced, but he cannot believe that this is the catalyst for most "pre-
mature" employee exits. After all, people who join a consulting firm
know that extended travel and long hours are the norm, especially
early in a career.

As Jeff continues to toss and turn, he keeps coming back to issues of inadequate coaching and feedback. He fears that the poor

development of direct reports may be a systemic problem. For example, he suspects that many new associates in their first and second years are not getting the on-the-job coaching and feedback that they need. He worries that this may ultimately impact their client relationships negatively. He also knows that in an industry like biotech, where everyone knows everyone else, all it takes is one blown client assignment and the firm's reputation can be damaged for years.

As Jeff considers the firm's reputation, he begins to focus on external issues as well, especially the question of how best to align the firm's organization with its increasingly competitive markets. Organized by industry practices—financial services, technology, and biotechnology—the firm has a historical growth pattern that involved adding industry groups to the mix. Naturally, sales have revolved around industry-focused teams, and much of the firm's reputation is grounded in its deep industry experience. Its actual offerings, however, are based on three service lines: (1) strategy and competitive analysis; (2) organization and change management; and (3) operations management. Each of these service lines has a different staffing model, a different practice economics, and a different labor pool.

In the middle of the night, much more so than in the light of day, Jeff recognizes that this structure is producing a major disconnect within the firm. Associates hired into the strategy practice often resent having to work on organization studies, and those hired into operations consulting have much more in common with each other than with the other consultants in their industry-based groups. Strains are showing in the matrix, and some partners believe that the firm should reorganize itself along the three service lines of strategy, organization and change management, and operations management with industries like technology and biotechnology overlays. The industry-based structure is a conundrum, however, because it has served the partners well, and no doubt it contributes to their industry depth and high utilization rates as people move around within each industry group as needed, regardless of their service line specialty.

At a more basic level, Jeff knows that underlying the organization issue is the question of what the firm's strategy should be for positioning itself in its markets. Increasingly, they find themselves competing with international strategy consulting firms, such as McKinsey & Company, Bain & Company, and Boston Consulting Group, for medium-size clients, especially in the biotech and technology industries, and with major management consulting firms like Booz Allen and Accenture in their operations and organization practices. Like many leaders of midsized professional service firms (PSFs), Jeff is worried about the firm being caught in a squeeze between the large global firms and the more narrowly focused boutiques. What does this mean for how his firm should position itself? Should its industry expertise become *more* or *less* important as a differentiating factor? And what does this "squeezing" from large and small firms mean for the structure?

Jeff berates himself and his partners for being like the proverbial shoeless shoemaker. They are a firm filled with strategy consultants, but no one has really spent much time analyzing whether the firm should reposition itself. His own process of becoming managing partner while also transitioning his former responsibilities and continuing to handle clients has left him with very little time for the longer-term issues that he knows he should be addressing now. Operating on overload, he should cut back on client work. Nonetheless, he continues to be the lead partner on three of the firm's largest accounts. As a practical matter, the clients have insisted on it. They are important clients that need and deserve his attention. Moreover, on a personal level, he really enjoys client interactions, especially working with case teams to craft client solutions and help the client's top managers as they wrestle to implement changes. He is also very effective at pitching new accounts—and with that thought he reminds himself that he has less than four hours before he has to rise and get ready for the flight to Los Angeles.

More than anything else, Jeff wishes he had more time to devote to critical issues facing the firm. One solution, batted about by the partners, has been to name a full-time chief operating officer who has no client responsibilities. Of course, such a recommendation might turn into a political football within the firm; almost all the partners complain about too little time and too much responsibility. There is no lack of healthy egos at the firm, and Jeff can envision the power struggles that selecting a full-time COO might set off. Eventually, Jeff falls asleep. Of course, his dreams are all about work.

Why a Fresh Leadership Approach Is Mandatory

Why is Jeff struggling with his leadership position? In large part, because he "inherited" a set of beliefs and a structure for running a professional service firm that are no longer completely valid. Balancing producer and manager roles has always been a challenge, but in today's marketplace it has become overwhelming. Trying to deal with this balancing act by putting one hat on and taking one hat off throughout the day is mentally and physically exhausting.

For this reason, we believe that an *integrated* leadership model is critical. This new model posits that leaders must stop thinking in terms of having two separate roles—usually one that they love and the other that they feel obligated to perform—and instead start thinking about overarching behaviors that are integral to who they are as leaders. With this new framework, they won't have to engage in Jeff's constant and enervating internal debates about how to allocate his time and energy. More to the point, understanding what these behaviors are and how they function will facilitate making the tough decisions Jeff and every professional service firm leader face daily. Setting a clear direction, spending time getting professionals committed to the direction, and executing are behaviors that are essential to the success of leaders in professional services. As we'll see, they provide guidance for leaders who feel overwhelmed by and understaffed for the tasks at hand.

Since Jay Lorsch and Peter Mathias wrote their seminal article about the "producing-manager" in 1987 and David Maister wrote *Managing the Professional Service Firm* in 1993, much has changed.[1] Despite the excellent models proffered by Lorsch and Mathias, and then Maister and others over the years, the professional service firm environment has changed sufficiently to warrant a new leadership model. The pressure to commoditize services requires a redefinition of Maister's three practice segments, procedural, gray hair, and rocket scientist.[2] Dealing with increasingly demanding clients, a loss of talent, and many other factors makes it necessary for firm leaders to expand their roles beyond Lorsch and Mathias's producer-manager standard. In short, we need to rethink and reformulate what leadership means in a professional service firm. In chapter 2, we will present what we call the "integrated" model, one that posits four critical activities for PSF leadership. Setting direction, getting commitment, executing, and setting a personal example are the essential activities that comprise our leadership model.

First, however, we want to make the case for the changing environment that makes this new leadership framework essential.

Size, Stress, and a Virtual, Global Marketplace

Much more now than in years past, leaders feel overloaded and conflicted most of the time.[3] No matter what these leaders do, they think they should be doing something else. And while these leaders worry, another associate leaves, or a partner feels disenfranchised or that he is not getting enough attention or recognition for what he is doing. Senior partners realize that they have not created a succession planning process throughout the organization. As they become aware that there are too many individuals on the list for promotion to partner, they worry about the economic implications for the firm if all are promoted.

Firm leaders are attempting to handle these issues by being good producers and managers, but these roles are insufficient given all the emerging pressures and problems. You can be the best producer and manager in the world and still experience a talent drain that robs the firm of its best and brightest people.

In addition to these stresses, firm leaders face significant leadership challenges due to emerging trends and events:

- *The pressure to maximize shareholder wealth.* Although this pressure has always existed, it has intensified in an era of increased competition and narrower margins. Arthur Andersen's management responded poorly to this pressure when working for Enron and destroyed its business as a result. No doubt other firm leaders have cut corners or compromised their values for the sake of maximum shareholder wealth. Large, publicly traded organizations feel the hot breath of Wall Street on their necks, and they in turn intensify their demands on professional service firms. At the same time, some publicly traded PSFs are desperate to increase billable hours, trying every trick in the book . . . and some that aren't. The temptation to overbill is powerful. Leaders are struggling to find the line between aggressive but ethical business practices and unethical ones. At times, it is a tough line to see, let alone toe.

- *Better informed and more demanding clients.* The gentleman's agreement between service firms and clients has weakened and, in some cases, disappeared entirely. It used to be that most clients trusted their firms' expertise implicitly and rarely questioned bills. Today, clients know more and are willing to act on that knowledge. They may challenge a firm's recommendations and push them to do more and better work in less time. This raises the performance bar in firms, and professionals may break or run in the face of what seems like unrealistic client demands. In addition, these tougher requirements often mandate greater accountability in terms of the way professionals spend time and money. This means more paperwork and working under greater scrutiny, neither of which help morale.

- *Failed professional service firm mergers.* USWeb/March FIRST, Morgan Stanley Dean Witter, and A.T. Kearney and Mitchell Madison are examples of mergers that at first seemed to be good ideas. However, on closer examination, the cultures were so different that the leaders of these partnerships could not bring about internal alignment in order to serve clients more effectively. The leaders were unable to turn outward and focus on clients when the internal factions pulled at the core of the firms.

- *The movement of industrial organizations into the professional services arena.* Nearly without exception, acquisitions of PSFs by large product-producing firms have failed, including such major attempts as IBM's acquisition of PricewaterhouseCoopers Consulting, CapGemini's acquisition of Ernst & Young Consulting, as well as CSC's early acquisition of Index Group. As organizations make strategic decisions about how to compete globally, leaders must decide whether to acquire, merge, or use an alliance, and how to manage these complex relationships.

- *Competition.* Many established partners have left big firms to set up their own smaller firms. This creates a more competitive landscape in all professional service arenas. Many firms are trying to differentiate themselves with less and less success. There seems to be a "sameness" among many PSFs due to increased competition in the market.

- *Demanding associates.* To complicate the challenges facing leaders in PSFs, associates have become more insistent. In some cases, they have only joined a PSF for a few years before looking for "more interesting work." Associates also have higher expectations for a work-life balance, engaging work, and consistent, ongoing feedback.

- *Fewer tight-knit partnerships.* Partner groups are not as close as they used to be. Part of this relates to the size of firms and to changing demographics and expectations, and part to an increase in demands placed on partners to bill time, recruit, meet aggressive revenue targets, deal with increased compliance, and manage other administrative responsibilities. Few partners reflect on how much they value the close relationships they once enjoyed within their firms.

- *The outsourcing trend.* Outsourcing offers firms the chance to take on potentially lucrative new projects and assignments formerly handled in-house. However, there is little evidence that advisory-based PSFs have been successful at outsourcing without losing their advisory presence, with many such firms suffering serious margin erosion and steep declines in profitability.

Our Perspective and Purpose

We have seen professional service firms moving in the direction of a new leadership model, and we want to help guide them toward this goal. They are engaged in a process of transformation in order to create improved results and work environments. For this transformation be as effective as possible, however, requires a framework tailored to the issues that professional service firms are confronting today.

We have also observed organizations where leaders were afraid to make any changes, even though they were losing ground to competitors on a daily basis. Many times, the heads of these organizations were stuck in the old leadership paradigm. They were effectively ignoring their associates by not having honest career development conversations. They were taking the wrong approach to performance appraisals and processes, such as ignoring the abusive behaviors of a few of their rainmakers because they couldn't give up the economic benefits. The leaders of these organizations had also perfected the process of writing superb mission statements that meant nothing in reality to the professionals within the firms. Years ago, these errors might not have had a devastating effect on their firms. Leaders could set poor examples and fail to secure commitment to the firm's purpose, and they still might do fine. Today, the impact of these mistakes is calamitous.

Professionals who self-select into these firms are very smart in their specific field of expertise, but may not be aware of organizational dynamics, the organizational practices that create aligned organizations, or the individual motivations of other professionals. In short, they are not yet integrated leaders. Despite sometimes limited leadership expertise, they feel confident in giving opinions on a wide range of organizational topics that may or may not help their firm operate more efficiently. We hope the chapters that follow will help these smart people make better management decisions using an integrated approach.

2

The Integrated Leader

Beyond the Producer-Manager Model

To meet new challenges of leadership, firms must adapt traditional philosophies and models. Traditional approaches do not have to be discarded entirely, but they must be adjusted to current realities. As we saw in the previous chapter, firms are fighting battles on many fronts, from dealing with sharper, more demanding clients to retaining their best people over time. Firm leaders have traditionally juggled their producer and manager roles, both to keep getting the work done and to motivate and grow associates. However, balancing these roles has become much more difficult in the current environment, which is volatile and intensely competitive, so we would like to pose an alternative to this increasingly challenging juggling act.

The integrated model of professional service firm leadership is evolutionary rather than revolutionary. It recognizes that the leadership challenge is now more important than ever, particularly as we observe many PSFs being both underled and undermanaged. Given the project-based and client-driven nature of PSFs, there is an intense ebb and flow within the firm as teams form, dissolve, and reform while new work is won and engagements are finished. This means that leaders must focus on making sure projects are completed effectively, profitably, and on time. Our leadership model also assumes that firms can no longer take their strategic direction for granted: the changes in their competitive environment demand a stronger sense of direction. In addition, we have created this model knowing that most firms are struggling to motivate their highly autonomous and high-need-for-achievement personalities over time, and to keep growing numbers of such people attracted to firm work. An emphasis on motivation, however, doesn't subordinate execution—the model recognizes that executing the work will continue to be central to PSFs and their leaders. Finally, our leadership framework rests on the belief that what leaders say and do is more important than ever, and that their behavior has ramifications for every aspect of the firm.

The Four Leadership Activities

The integrated leadership model is based on extensive observation of effective leaders in a wide range of PSFs. These include consulting, investment banking, public accounting, the law, investment management, public relations, advertising, academic institutions, and the medical profession. It is also based on years of observation of *ineffective* leaders. They are often excellent professionals, but as leaders they seem unable to create a clear sense of direction, inspire others, or get results; or if they do get results, they are attained at great organizational and human cost. Typically, ineffective leaders are professionals whom others hate to work for, even though they may be highly regarded experts in their field. In contrast, excellent PSF leaders create a sense of purpose and a clear focus on execution, while supporting and gaining the commitment of their people. As a result, they develop teams and work cultures that attract top people who want to grow and do an outstanding job.

The leadership framework we propose is activity-based in that it deals with distinctly observable actions. It describes actual, observable behaviors that leaders may learn to become more effective. The model consists of four distinct but highly interrelated sets of leadership activities:

- *Setting direction.* PSFs often focus on the short term and spend little time providing direction on where the firm or practice is going and why. Since professionals are often solely focused on specific goals and tasks, they need leaders to articulate the organization's objectives and how their work relates to those objectives. Setting direction keeps everyone eyeing the same target and minimizes false starts and wasted effort. It is important in all organizations but critical in PSFs, especially at a time when associates and partners are moving in and out of firms at a surprising rate or are under so much pressure that they don't grasp where the firm is heading.

- *Gaining commitment to the direction.* As we describe in chapter 3, professionals have an innate need to be involved and included. They want to be heard. Unfortunately, a sense of alienation exists among firm professionals at all levels who feel the firm has changed and that the current culture and leadership has left them out; many solid performers who are not the star players at a firm often feel as if their contributions are being undervalued. When professionals feel excluded—or that no efforts are made to solicit their ideas and objections—they feel alienated and fail to focus on the task at hand. Many will pull away from other professionals and become cynical. Over time, some professionals may actually sabotage firm goals if they do not feel committed to the desired outcomes. Gaining commitment increases the odds that people will work harder and more creatively to move a firm, practice, or project in the desired direction.

- *Execution.* Follow-through and accountability cannot be left to chance, even though professionals are naturally task-driven. Execution is a key activity for leaders who are intimately involved in business development, selling, client service, and delivery. Balancing the need to get things done with the need to get professionals on board is a huge challenge for PSF leadership. Execution is about not letting dates slide. Execution is the process of meeting the financial goals that have been set and holding professionals at all levels accountable.

- *Setting a personal example.* Providing a positive personal example is crucial when leading professionals. In the stress-filled, volatile environments of PSFs, it matters what leaders actually do through word and deed. Leaders must embody the firm's stated values and goals or those values and goals become meaningless for professionals. Gaining commitment requires that leaders display personal integrity, support their professionals, and take responsibility for their own actions—including mistakes. Nothing undermines the credibility of leaders as quickly as exhorting professionals to do one thing while they themselves do the opposite.

These four sets of leadership behaviors form what we term the integrated leadership model for PSFs. Figure 2-1 provides a visual description of how direction, commitment, and execution are the three *basic* leadership activities, with "personal example" at their center. As this figure suggests, these activities must be *integral* and *natural* aspects of managing professionals, projects, and practices in real time. Although the four leadership behaviors are distinct, they are also interrelated. Thus, firm leaders need to integrate all of them into their modus operandi. For instance, it isn't much use setting direction if one's personal example doesn't reinforce that direction. Building commitment is terrific, but it's worthless if execution of that commitment doesn't happen. In short, direction, commitment, execution, and personal example are not ancillary activities to doing the work, relegated to counseling sessions or pep talks. They are at the core of producing results.

FIGURE 2-1

The leaders' role in professional service firms

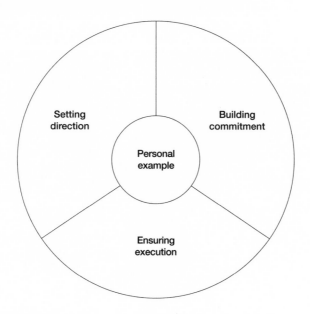

Source: Thomas J. DeLong.

Ideally, this integrated model will help leaders manage the conflicting requirements, intensifying client demands, and other stress-producing factors that make leading other professionals such a challenge. Instead of desperately swinging back and forth between producer and manager responsibilities, this model posits that these four overarching leadership behaviors will make being a leader a more feasible proposition. Leaders who integrate these behaviors will find themselves leading more efficiently and productively; these behaviors will help them prioritize their actions as well as make decisions.

The integrated leadership model is a frame to guide both long- and short-term activities. Rather than caroming from one urgent call to another short-term demand, leaders who have internalized this model into observable behaviors find that other professionals waste less time and instead focus on real challenges. The model provides a leader with both perspective and focus at the firm or practice level. With more focus, a leader wastes less time feeling guilty about what she is not doing. Rather, the leader feels more in control and strategic in words and deeds.

Let us examine each of these four activities in more detail, focusing on the leadership behaviors that comprise each dimension, how others have incorporated this model, and how all four components can be integrated to create effective leadership in a professional service firm.

Setting Direction

Professional service firms operate in fluid markets, causing them to seek a degree of certainty and stability in the midst of unpredictable and volatile events. They also tend to attract detail-oriented, focused individuals who work long and hard but who also want a sense of where their labors are taking them (and the firm). By setting direction, you provide the element of certainty and the road map your professionals seek.

At All Levels

At all levels of the firm, leaders must communicate a picture of the firm's future, a meaningful rationale for moving in this direction, and how the practice fits into this picture. This does not mean giving a short speech filled with generalities about a brighter future and a vague explanation of how to get there. Talking about how "we must expand our capabilities" or "become a leaner, more flexible firm" is akin to telling someone who is lost that he can find his destination by driving north. Rather, you need to communicate why a direction has been selected for the firm, practice, or group; who participated in creating it; and how it will be achieved.

Being able to do this, of course, presumes that the organization's leadership has thought through what that direction should be, either in terms of its positioning strategy for attaining competitive advantage, or in terms of its business model and underlying client-service proposition. Some firms philosophically concentrate on being internally focused when they hire the best professionals who then serve clients. We are speaking here about firms that start with the client in mind. Being clear on direction means being able to answer the following questions:

- How are we actually competing?

- Why are we succeeding (or not)?

- Who are our real competitors?

- Are we really different from our competitors?

- Are we encumbered or enhanced by our past performance, traditions, and history?

- How might changes in financial and labor markets affect how we approach and serve clients?

- Does our economic model hold up over time?

Answering these questions requires taking into account the states of current markets, economic trends, and how competitors are interpreting these and proceeding into the future. Above all, setting direction requires a clear articulation of the firm's strategy and purpose. Having a client-value proposition ensures that a firm is serving the type of client that is financially worthwhile to serve. This can also be a very powerful and tangible source of direction if leaders can articulate it clearly and communicate it widely. The client-value proposition is based on what the organization can do better than anyone else in its practice segment. In successful practices, it is what drives the business and economic model. If it is well understood by professionals, the client-value proposition can become a very powerful source of internalized direction that both guides and motivates actions on a daily basis. If your professionals really understand and believe in your client-value proposition, it can be both a rallying cry when the business cycle gets challenging and a touchstone for what the right thing to do is. But this requires that leaders actively communicate what types of clients are being served and the economics that support serving that client in a particular way over and over. Few firm leaders communicate the direction often enough. Many leaders believe everyone understands the direction but professionals need reassurance time and again.

Don't underestimate the difficulty of communicating a clear, concise direction.[1] We often ask professionals we are working with whether their people could pass the following elevator test: upon entering an elevator in the lobby of your building, state in general terms the strategy, purpose, or goal of your firm before the elevator stops at your floor. Passing the test requires that the strategy/purpose/goal statement matches how the majority of employees perceive these issues. Our experience reveals that few organizations pass the test. In fact, when we give this test to organizational leaders, we are frequently greeted with blank stares or questions:

"What do you mean by the firm's 'direction'?"

"How did my colleagues respond to the test?"

"What are you really looking for? Is there a right answer?"

This exercise underscores the importance of consensus, focus, and single-mindedness about an organization's direction and the way it is communicated. It is one thing to agree on direction (which is difficult enough), and quite another to have a collective conversation about what it means and how best to communicate that direction.

The very nature of professional service firms today makes it easy for professionals to lose sight of the firm's broader purpose and mission. Professionals frequently travel to client sites and are usually under intense pressure to meet ambitious (and sometimes ambiguous) client expectations. As a result, they are often physically or psychologically removed from headquarters. When leaders consistently remind their professionals of the unit's focus and goals, professionals can better align their efforts with the firm's direction and their unit's future efforts.

Setting direction also means defining objectives and measuring results at both a macro- and micro-level. Creating measurable objectives—around profits and performance—that align with long-term strategy (and/or your client-value proposition) is central to this process, but objectives must be clear and compelling. If they don't make sense to professionals throughout the firm, they won't be taken seriously. Professionals need more than short-term performance goals; they also need an idea of how the firm will measure mid- and long-term success. People are eager to ask, "What will success look like?" and "Will it be measured in relationship to other firms or to last year's efforts?"

Understandably, firm and practice leaders are often reluctant to articulate objectives and measures that will help drive the business in a unified direction because they fear that market changes will force them to make sudden departures in their strategies. They do not want to appear shortsighted or fickle, either to their own professionals or to those outside the firm. Setting direction can also involve explaining your strategy to other practice groups within the firm, especially those with which you are potentially interdependent.

Setting direction may entail creating or reinforcing a firm image or brand. Leading from the front—being visible in the community while leading professionals—and building a firm's reputation should not be seen as a political process but rather a "marketing" process in the best sense of that term. Ambiguity about the mission of a firm, division, or practice will generate confusion both internally and externally. Clients unable to discern differentiating and defining characteristics in what you do for them might wonder whether your organization really has anything unique to offer. They may wonder whether competitors' unflattering characterizations might be true. Likewise, professionals want the firm they come to work for each morning to stand out, to have a reputation that elicits a positive response from clients, friends, and colleagues employed elsewhere.

At the Operational Level

Giving direction at the operational level involves setting expectations and providing direction on a day-to-day, project-by-project basis. It consists of translating what the firm's or the practice's strategy means in terms of choices, decisions, and actions that are made in serving clients, as illustrated by the following suggested interactions.

- Explain to a case team why developing follow-on work after the project is completed is critical to successful implementation of the firm's recommendations; further explain why getting the follow-on work is important to the firm's penetration strategy.

- Resolve a dispute between two consultants by reminding them of how the firm's client-value proposition applies in determining what is important to consider in the particular situation.

- Explain why the firm is choosing *not* to propose on a particular project or deal in terms of the firm's positioning strategy, available resources, quality standards, margin targets, and so on.

- Find occasions to talk about the practice's priorities and targets, and describe how it is doing against its targets.

- Relate the positioning strategy to why the firm is winning new business.

Setting expectations and reinforcing firm priorities on a day-to-day basis contribute to effective leadership at the operational level. Without it, the best firm, division, and practice strategies are meaningless. Goals will be reached by accident. Good strategy is essential, but it is never a substitute for strong commitment and execution.

Providing effective leadership at the operational level also includes setting expectations and providing direction on operational issues. Consider the following examples:

- Get a deal team to settle on their action priorities quickly when a client has entered discussion with a competitor proposing a radically different structure for the transaction.

- Provide a new audit team senior manager who lacks experience in the client's industry with thoughtful and clear guidance about what aspects of the audit are different or especially important given the nature of the client's industry, and explain why.

- Touch base with a junior partner who is negotiating with a potential client on a complex project: give guidance concerning scope, terms, and fees, and ensure that you are available as the negotiation progresses over a day or two.

- Frame the client situation for a newly formed case team: describe in actionable terms what the client views as the critical issues, the composition of the client team, who the key players are, and how they differ on their perceptions of the problems.

These are all examples of the kind of direction that comprises leadership on the ground—where the real work gets done. Although most professionals prize their autonomy and hate being micromanaged, this type of direction gives them a sense of what's salient and of where "we," collectively, are headed and why. If you think about your own experience, you may recall that there is nothing as frustrating as being in the dark about what really matters in an engagement, or wasting a lot of valuable time doing work that turns out to be useless or irrelevant because your leader failed to clue you in.

At a time when some firms are expanding rapidly, others are merging, and still others are going through major restructuring, professionals may feel that their work is disconnected from the firm's purpose. With higher turnover rates for supervisors who are here today and gone tomorrow, associates may lack the consistent presence providing a sense that their efforts are contributing to a firm's goals. As firms shift strategies in response to complex global changes or emerging competitive pressures, professionals may be uncertain what these shifts mean for them at a micro level.

For all these reasons, providing ongoing direction at the operational level is crucial.

Building Commitment

Some professional service firms do a good job of setting direction but a poor job of obtaining buy-in and commitment to that direction. In a business where employees are more acquiescent and less involved in their work, such an approach might work. In the professional service field, however, professionals want to feel that they and the work they do matter to the firm. In fact, many professionals confess to sabotaging firm efforts when their leaders failed to involve them.

Autonomous, goal-oriented, and entrepreneurial, many professionals can fairly be characterized as rugged individualists. Consequently, they relish working alone but also expect their leaders to involve them in important processes. This does not mean that professionals want to take on more responsibility but that they want to give input. On high-stake questions, partner-level professionals demand to be part of the input process. They want to be included but not told how to do their work. This paradox is what makes the role of leader in a PSF so challenging.

Of the four core leadership activities of our leadership model, commitment is often perceived as the least important but it is just as crucial. Securing commitment means consciously paying attention and spending time on keeping professionals connected to the firm and its work, an expenditure that many driven professionals often deem wasteful. As we have noted, leaders in PSFs often feel pushed and pulled to achieve results under time pressure. When this happens, they tend to view anything outside of client activities as superfluous. Under these circumstances, it is easy to see why setting direction and ensuring execution can eclipse gaining commitment as leadership priorities. Leaders in such firms fail to see that without widespread commitment to the firm's direction, professionals often lose focus on key objectives, especially during pressure-filled, volatile periods. When competition gets tough, when professionals are asked to work long hours under intense pressure, or when headhunters are haunting your halls, commitment helps professionals maintain their focus.

At the Firm Level

At the firm or practice level, commitment exists when professionals feel deeply identified and connected with the firm, its work, and what the firm stands for. Inspiration begets commitment. Professionals are inspired by knowing why they come to work and why they work the number of hours they do. Most important, they want to know that someone senior to them knows in a meaningful way that they are doing good work. Professionals most often leave firms because they believe they are no longer central to the mission of the firm; they are uninspired. They quickly lose confidence and their trust erodes. Professionals, notwithstanding their need for considerable autonomy, want leaders who create a compelling vision for the firm, who paint motivating pictures of the future, and who connect with them personally.

Commitment flows from a clear, concise direction, and it also flows from trust. People buy into the direction that the firm is heading when they trust their leadership. Trust can be built one hundred and one ways, through both small and large actions. For instance, professionals need to be assured that promotion and compensation

26

committees are staffed by competent, trusted professionals who have devised fair systems and processes.

As we noted earlier, professionals must see alignment between what leaders say and what they do. It is much easier for professionals to commit to a firm's purpose and values when leaders *at all levels* demonstrate that the firm's goals are worthy of that commitment. The tension between adhering to espoused values—what the firm says it believes in—and the pressure to attain results can often fray the bond of trust between leaders and professionals.[2] In the professional service arena, where high performers are elevated to star status, leaders sometimes make decisions that erode trust and fray commitment to a given direction.

In the Harvard Business School case study "Rob Parson at Morgan Stanley," the protagonist joins the firm with the intention of transforming a business, being promoted to managing director, and making his mentor and boss Paul Nasr proud of the decision to hire him.[3] Parson pushes his direct reports hard for results to the point of being seen as abusive. At the same time, John Mack is trying to change the culture of Morgan Stanley, focusing on treating people with dignity and respect. The climactic moment in the case comes when Parson's boss, Nasr, must decide whether to recommend Parson for promotion based on his stellar performance, even though he has consistently crossed the line on some of the firm's core values.

Similar dilemmas challenge all leaders in firms that operate in highly competitive markets with highly competitive professionals. In the case of Rob Parson, senior management told Nasr that Parson wouldn't be put on the promotion list. Leaders willing to compromise the firm's values to keep a high-performing "star" satisfied, or to deal with the emergency of the moment, ignore the professionals who adhere to the firm's values while rewarding the super-producers who do not. The fallout: increased cynicism and diminished commitment to the firm and its values.

Another very important source of both commitment and trust is whether professionals have the sense of being included and "in the know." There are too many examples to cite of partnerships that have unraveled when partners lost a sense of inclusion and trust in the firm's leadership.

The power of feeling connected and included cannot be overestimated. For example, after years of hearing about a highly profitable and prestigious law firm, we were invited to work with the firm on some governance and organizational issues. Partners at rival firms who had spent their associate years there almost always described the firm with admiration, commenting on its high standards and the commitment of its partners. Shortly after beginning to work with the firm, we were invited to attend one of its quarterly, "all hands" partners' meetings, which the managing partner felt was critical to the firm's effectiveness. When we heard about these meetings, at first we were skeptical (have you ever met a professional who loves meetings?)—until we attended one. Our first observation was that there was broad attendance from all departments. As many senior partners attended as did younger partners. One of the topics for the day was a review of the past year's financials. Budgets were discussed and practice business plans reviewed. The topics were not particularly scintillating. However, there was no eye-rolling behavior from the two hundred or so partners assembled. They were listening, asking questions, and engaged in intense give-and-take.

At the conclusion of the meeting, to our surprise, the partners stood up and applauded. There was a sense of community and engagement. Having worked with this firm, we can assure you that these partners are not a servile group, willing to obey at a moment's notice. They have opinions about everything from office space to law school recruiting to changes in their legal markets. Like anyone else, however, they value being kept abreast of the major competitive, financial, and operational issues facing the firm. It was apparent that they felt deeply connected to the firm and included on relevant issues that mattered. We found it fascinating that of two hundred twenty furiously busy partners, all but a dozen attended the meeting, either in person or by videoconference. We later learned that this level of attendance was typical. "You miss one only if you're in the middle of a transaction or in court," commented one partner. It was clear to us why the managing partner saw the quarterly meeting as critical to creating a strong sense of partnership.

Granted, gaining the commitment of two hundred twenty partners is an easier task than winning the commitment of six thousand professionals around the globe. Our observation has been, however, that even very large firms are able to gain high levels of commitment by creating vehicles through which key people stay involved and connected. Examples abound of firms like McKinsey & Company, Bain & Company, Egon Zehnder International, and Linklaters (to mention just a few) that use similar types of meetings to foster a sense of cohesion and commitment among partners and professionals. They do so because it makes a difference in who wins and who loses.

There are many other tools and behaviors that you can use to build commitment at the firm and practice levels. Adhering to values, building trust, involving key people in important decisions, and recognizing "right" behavior combine for a synergistic effect, one that powerfully conveys leadership's sincerity and belief in the firm's goals. Leaders ignore these actions at their peril. Professionals who are not inspired to commit to a common direction often end up sabotaging efforts to do so. Commitment to a common direction may not sound like a leadership priority, but it is.

Recognize, too, that we live and work in an era where cynicism, irony, and pessimism are more prevalent than ever before, especially among young professionals. They are quick to suspect the worst and adopt a skeptical mentality. No doubt the widespread downsizing trends and corporate scandals have fueled these negative attitudes.

When leaders build commitment to a common direction, however, they offer a potential antidote to such poisonous assumptions. As they fully engage the hearts and minds of their people, they help create positive, inclusive outlooks that generate tremendous effort and enthusiasm—that greatly benefit firms.

At the Operational Level

Gaining commitment at the operational level involves inspiring, motivating, and connecting with your professionals *on a personal basis*. Again, this is part of the leadership that occurs to get work done on a day-to-day basis. It includes building trust, communicating the firm's values, and explicitly recognizing people for doing "the right thing." Consider, for example, the following suggested interactions:

- Stop an associate in the hallway and take the time to congratulate him on winning a new engagement or deal.

- Send a quick e-mail to a very promising third-year associate who has just done an outstanding job on an important aspect of a matter; then, briefly comment on it again the next time you see her. (Think back to when you were in her situation and how it left you feeling if a partner commended you in that way.)

- Take the time to acknowledge people in the course of work—even a quick "Hello, how's it going?" in the hallway.

- Provide your professionals with all kinds of recognition for good work, from formal recognition during a meeting to sticking your head into a professional's office for thirty seconds and saying, "What a great job you guys did on the X account." This takes very little time—a matter of seconds—but it does require an ongoing awareness of the power of recognition in gaining commitment.

- Take an analyst who has put a huge amount of time into completing material for a major portion of a client presentation to the presentation itself. (Recently, one of our clients not only took the analyst to the presentation but actually had him make part of the presentation. How committed do you think that left the analyst feeling?)

- Take the time to tell a senior associate that you are aware that she's been working long hours on fairly standard, repetitive work, that you value her commitment, and that you will do all that you can to get her assigned to some more interesting projects as soon as possible.

- Give credit to others. Giving credit is a great way of gaining commitment, while hogging credit is a sure way of losing commitment.

- Recognize people for doing the "right thing" in a given situation. Take aside and compliment a deal team leader who has just given a third-year associate careful and constructive feedback on an aspect of a transaction that needs to be redone.

- Take time to include three of your key reports on an important decision concerning the group that will affect their work for the next three months.

- Be aware of when your own actions, lack of planning, or procrastination has resulted in a pile of work being dumped on your people that has to be "done yesterday." Most professionals are smart enough to see this behavior when it is a pattern, even if you yourself don't see it. When they do see it, they deeply resent it. It's a commitment killer, and you have to develop the discipline to stop doing it.

- Create an occasion (even a small one) to celebrate the successful completion of an important deal, project, or matter that your people have gone all out to complete.

With very few exceptions, all of the above examples concern actions that take no more than a minute or two, and many only a matter of seconds. Yet they are powerful behaviors for motivating professionals and making them feel valued, connected, and part of an effort that matters. They are also actions that can be naturally incorporated into the day-to-day interactions of getting the work done. What they do require, however, is having an awareness that gaining commitment is an integral aspect of leadership on a daily basis. It is this awareness that will enable you to see and act on the many opportunities that exist for gaining commitment in the normal course of doing the job.

We began this section by describing the many ways that commitment can be built at the firm and practice levels. Let us end it by saying that these actions are never substitutes for what a firm's partners, managing directors, and other leaders actually do on an operational basis day in and day out. Ultimately it is their actions that will either gain or lose the commitment of your professionals.

Ensuring Execution

Execution plays to the strength of task-driven professionals who self-select into professional service firms. It also plays to their weakness, in that they often become consumed by the tasks at hand and lose sight of the bigger picture. Execution is especially salient for leaders who are managers *and* producers. As producers they are themselves intimately involved in the execution of work for clients, while as managers they are accountable for what others accomplish. The role of leadership, then, is to define and inspire execution in sufficiently broad terms to ensure that work gets done synergistically and not in isolation. Professionals may execute as individuals but not on teams; they may accomplish short-term tasks but assign low priorities to long-term responsibilities. They may obsess over their part of the deal but lose sight of the total transaction. They may focus on activities that enhance their practice while seriously undermining the well-being of the firm. Effective leadership serves as a preventive measure for such potential problems.

At the Firm Level

Execution at the firm or practice group level ensures that the firm's or practice's strategies, priorities, and plans are actually implemented and acted upon; that those responsible for different divisions, practice groups, or other units meet their business plans and objectives. Oftentimes this means that leadership has to be relentless and persistent in attaining a long-term objective.

Bruce Jamerson, a former investment banker at Credit Suisse, is an excellent example in his determined pursuit of a strategically targeted account—Union Carbide Corporation.[4] He knew that Morgan Stanley had been the primary banker for decades, yet over a period of a couple of years he met continually with Union Carbide executives. When the company subsequently looked for assistance, and Morgan Stanley decided not to float a bridge loan, Jamerson and Credit Suisse jumped at the opportunity. The relationship between Morgan Stanley and Union Carbide was never the same again, and for the next ten years Union Carbide was one of Credit Suisse's important clients. This is just one example of determined execution in achieving a strategic goal and then delivering on the client-value proposition.

Executing direction means assembling teams of professionals who are committed to the firm's strategies for creating and delivering client value and then ensuring that they do so. The challenge for leadership is that many professionals are not natural team players. They want autonomy. Intent on traveling from point A to point B in the shortest time, they resent participation in any group that lengthens the time needed to complete their individual tasks. Leaders in PSFs often find themselves swimming upstream in their attempts to create teams capable of executing the firm's direction. They can motivate professionals to execute effectively on teams, however, if they recognize and address the issues that are encouraging "me-first" behaviors.

Several years ago, the managing partner of a firm we were working with was in the process of bringing new leaders onto the operating committee. Team members, leery of one another, sought to stake out positions based on old relationships or old territories. The operating committee meetings were less than effective, and its members struggled to devise a competitive strategy they could all agree on.

Concurrently, the firm was developing its first formalized performance evaluation process for professionals. Seeing this as an opportunity, the managing partner informed the operating committee that as part of this process, they would be evaluating each other. The evaluations would impact compensation and their level of responsibility in the firm. When they realized this, the individuals on the committee began to share information and informally discuss firm challenges. They began to work together more collaboratively in anticipation of the day of reckoning on which they would evaluate and be evaluated by one another. Despite their inclination to work individually, these committee members executed as a team when they were motivated to do so.

Executing direction also requires leaders to focus attention on creating and delivering client value. As a leader in a professional service firm, you can never forget that this is a firm's raison d'être and never let your people forget it. They must be able to respond to the question that clients ask often and explicitly: "Are you giving the best service by the best professionals for the best value?"

At the Operational Level

Execution at the operational level is all about ensuring that the client's total needs are met—on time, on budget, and on point in terms of the quality of deliverables and service. It is also about ensuring that goals are met in winning new engagements, market segment penetration, and growth. In a word, it is also about ensuring that you and your group "hit its numbers." More specifically it consists of:

- delivering and enhancing client value;

- assembling the right people and teams;

- ensuring that goals are met and results are attained; and

- touching base with your people on how projects or matters are progressing.

Executing also means developing your professionals. Whether it is investment banking, accounting, or the law, professionals have a reflexive need for learning, growth, and development as well as for mentors who can facilitate this process. This is especially the case in these firms because they all operate on an apprenticeship model. Associates join firms anticipating that their skills will be developed through assignments that stretch their capacities. When these expectations are not met, the unwritten covenant between the professional and the firm is broken. This broken pact diminishes their

35

motivation, and as a result execution suffers. Unfortunately, people frequently report that introductory training sessions were the only formal training they ever received, even if they were with a firm for as long as ten years.

While most training is on the job in firms that are stratified apprenticeships, professionals want the assurance that an organization, both in its mission and operationally, cares about the development of its people. All firms say that they develop key individuals, but few PSFs deliver on this promise in a methodical, organized way.

The challenge for leaders is to develop professionals throughout their tenure with the firm. Many junior professionals are bored after doing the same thing month after month, and many of them lose their edge, which diminishes their ability to execute. Ultimately, the purpose of execution is to generate financial results by meeting client needs. It is to this end that leaders need to develop their people and organize them into effective teams capable of creating and delivering client value.

PSFs that execute with excellence turn their clients into great referral sources and all-around boosters. The value of a firm's brand is enhanced as clients tell others about the quality of work delivered by the firm and its professionals. The opposite, of course, is also true. Clients who believe that the value proposition was not satisfied will readily tell others that the firm didn't execute, making it more difficult for the firm to secure new clients.

As you can tell, we are defining execution in much broader terms than firm leaders may have done in the past. A decade ago, the focus was primarily on short-term results, and that worked for many firms. Today, firms cannot survive unless they execute with the aim of achieving both short- and long-term goals. Firms cannot compete successfully unless they execute from both the producer and manager perspectives. It is just as important to make sure people are developed as it is to meet client expectations.

Above all else, creating and delivering client value is the cornerstone of high-performing professional service firms. Holding professionals accountable for results can be difficult. Having difficult conversations about goals that are not achieved is the toughest task for professionals in PSFs. If you fail to execute based on this fundamental principle, none of the other essential behaviors will hold up for the long term.

The Power of Personal Example

Leaders have many ways to set direction, secure commitment, and increase execution effectiveness. Through one-on-one discussions and talks to larger groups, they can communicate the importance of these three core activities. Leaders are most likely to influence their people through personal example, however (see figure 2-2). Of all the dimensions of the integrated leadership model, the cornerstone is the power of personal example. The higher a leader is in a firm's hierarchy, the more scrutiny he or she will experience. When a managing partner who rarely leaves his corner office exhorts his partners to call more often on clients between projects or transactions, his professionals will see an obvious disconnect between this leader's words and actions. Professionals are quick to spot this type of gap and discuss it disparagingly with colleagues behind closed doors.

Other actions could include:

- Following through with assignments so everyone at the firm knows you follow through and that you hold others accountable.

- Giving honest and direct (but nonpunishing) feedback behind closed doors when one of your direct reports is out of line.

FIGURE 2-2

Producing-managing-leading framework

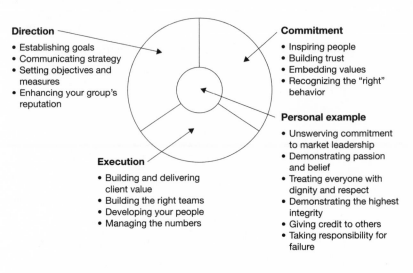

Direction
- Establishing goals
- Communicating strategy
- Setting objectives and measures
- Enhancing your group's reputation

Commitment
- Inspiring people
- Building trust
- Embedding values
- Recognizing the "right" behavior

Personal example
- Unswerving commitment to market leadership
- Demonstrating passion and belief
- Treating everyone with dignity and respect
- Demonstrating the highest integrity
- Giving credit to others
- Taking responsibility for failure

Execution
- Building and delivering client value
- Building the right teams
- Developing your people
- Managing the numbers

Source: Thomas J. DeLong.

- Praising when appropriate but not lavishing uncalled-for admiration.

- Taking a pay cut before the rank-and-file professionals have their pay reduced.

- Creating an atmosphere where performance counts more than politics.

- Interacting with colleagues so that they leave feeling inspired, rather than bullied.

The most powerful connection between leaders and professionals is achieved through face-to-face interaction.[5] Too often leaders pass up opportunities to influence their people in meaningful ways by minimizing this type of interaction. Instead, they rely on phone, e-mail, and fax to communicate, failing to take advantage of opportunities to set a personal example.

One leader we know was so focused on running her research division that she didn't even acknowledge her colleagues and professionals as they passed her in the office corridors. She did not intend to communicate disinterest or to be perceived as rude by her colleagues, and she certainly didn't mean to be seen as either arrogant or stressed. She was unaware of how she was being perceived and evaluated by others, and it hurt her credibility as a leader.

High-achieving producing managers are often so focused on crossing the next task off their lists that they often neglect their people. This focus on getting short-term results often comes at the cost of not taking the time to connect with people one-on-one or in groups. Often, market forces dictate longer working hours, exhausting travel schedules, and solitary assignments away from headquarters, all of which adversely affect the work cultures of professional service firms. The result is that many PSFs lack friendly, supportive environments. Indeed, some border on being professional sweatshops, even though the pay is considerable. In firms like this, leaders who consistently make unrealistic demands of their professionals rationalize their behavior by saying that they are under pressure precipitated by client demands. Effective leaders can mitigate the negative impact of such peak periods by communicating to their professionals that they are not alone, that what they are doing matters to the firm, and that professionals need to support one another over the long term.

Most leaders in PSFs have struggled with the dilemma of how to deal with highly productive star performers who are indifferent to or abusive of their professionals. Should stars whose behavior is at variance with firm values be promoted? Should they be awarded bonuses to motivate them to generate even higher profits? Many leaders reluctantly choose short-term profits and refrain from making the tough decision to confront dysfunctional behavior that runs contrary to firm values.

Professionals expect leaders to exhibit integrity and consistency in word and deed, and rewarding abusive stars thwarts these expectations. Professionals also expect the processes leaders put in place to be equitable and objective.

Narayana Murthy, chairman emeritus of Infosys Technologies, personifies leading by example. He is not perfect—he can be stubborn and get angry, and he may not be the most inspirational speaker. Yet you know that he is authentic to the core. He provides the ultimate personal example of doing what he believes. Murthy felt so strongly about sharing the success of Infosys that he was the first CEO in India to give equity to his professionals. Infosys was also the first Indian company to be publicly traded in the United States. Perhaps even more astonishingly, he gives himself a paltry salary of $30,000 and has stated often that the best night's rest is one with a guilt-free conscience. After an interview with Murthy, people often note that they are in a reflective mood, asking themselves questions such as, "How are you measuring up as a person?" Murthy is honest, direct, and has very high expectations of professionals.

Great leaders also give other people credit.[6] They set the example of praising professionals not only for building client value and generating revenue but for being good communicators and relationship builders. Everyone needs frequent feedback, and leaders should make it their business to provide it across the board. The leader who sets an example of crediting or acknowledging work that has been completed or is in the pipeline will motivate professionals who might be questioning their own abilities or wondering whether all their effort is worth it. Giving credit costs nothing, but it does take effort, self-awareness, and an awareness of the situation at hand.

Perhaps even more challenging, leaders must take responsibility for their own failure and acknowledge their own mistakes. This type of personal example is seldom seen in PSFs. It may seem counterintuitive to highly successful, highly competitive leaders to admit to failures. When you own up to a bad call, your people know they can trust your honesty and it inspires them to follow suit. During the process of executing direction, there are bound to be mistakes, and it is far better to acknowledge them than to sweep them under the rug. When that is done, they tend to resurface and trip up the firm.

We have asked leaders in a number of firms to describe failures for which they were responsible that never came to light. A typical response was: "I'm sure I've made mistakes, but none stand out as remarkable. I'm far from perfect, but I don't have any stories to share." It's the rare and exceptional leader who is open about his mistakes and what he has learned from them. Typically, these leaders create learning cultures where creativity is rewarded and mistakes are acknowledged and corrected—thus leading to better practices and ultimately better client service.

Personal example is far more essential now than in the past, given the host of scandals at the beginning of this century. Firms and their leaders are under great scrutiny, and accountability is today's byword, especially when practices are seen as being too close to the ethical line. Leaders who inspire others through value consistency— by making sure their actions are consistent with their beliefs, both personally and professionally—will possess the extra edge of credibility that professionals can trust. To gain this edge, therefore, keep the following issues in mind.

While you are under constant pressure to meet firm expectations, client demands, and your own internal goals, you will be increasingly challenged to guide your professionals in a focused, directed way that enhances client value. In the face of a daily rash of crises, you need to maintain perspective and remain focused on what is important. Push yourself to ask tough, self-reflective questions about how you exhibit leadership through your personal conduct and behavior. The challenge has never been more daunting—or exciting. Take the opportunity to step back and assess your leadership style in terms of how well you are providing direction to your professionals; building commitment to the firm and its value proposition; ensuring quality execution; and serving as a role model in your personal example for the behaviors, values, and performance that you want from your professionals. The integrated leadership model is incomplete if any one of the four core behaviors is left out. The model is powerful only if leaders set direction, get commitment to the direction, execute, and by their actions set personal examples as leaders. Although the integrated model seems simple, the next chapter shows the challenges of following through on the four key behaviors when external and internal challenges mount for PSF leaders.

3

Professional Service Firms

A Breed Apart

Professional service firms and product-producing companies are similar, but different in certain key respects, especially from a leadership perspective. This characteristic of being "similar but different" can prove to be confusing to the untrained eye, because the differences may seem insignificant. In fact, these differences are more important than ever, making traditional leadership models even more out-of-date for PSFs. In addition, as the line between PSFs and corporations has begun to blur, some PSFs have adopted leadership models more appropriate for product-producing companies. Some firm professionals believe that their organizations behave in a more corporate manner because of their more complex structure and size. As a result, the growth of PSFs

43

has caused some firm leaders to adopt leadership and management approaches that are ill-suited to firm cultures and structures.

Many formerly modest-sized PSFs, such as law firms, engineering consulting firms, and accounting firms, are increasing rapidly in terms of size, scale, and complexity. Consequently, they are looking to the corporate model for answers. At the same time, many product-producing corporations are either considering adding professional services to their offerings or are already doing so, unaware of the critical differences between PSFs and their own organizations. This lack of awareness can result in disasters, as evidenced by IBM's great difficulties in integrating PricewaterhouseCoopers Consulting, CSC's long-term problems in integrating its acquisition of the Index Group (the top IT consulting firm of its era), and CapGemini's failure to successfully integrate Ernst & Young Consulting.

In this environment the wrong leadership model can do great damage to an otherwise healthy, growing professional service firm. Conversely, the right model can help achieve ambitious growth objectives. For these reasons, we want to suggest why the integrated leadership model is particularly effective and relevant today, especially given the crucial differences between PSFs and product-based corporations. We'll look at how providing direction, building commitment, ensuring execution, and setting a personal example are tailored to the specific requirements of PSF leadership. First, we want to clarify the major differences between PSFs and product-producing corporations, since it is only when these differences are understood that the value of a new leadership model becomes evident.

The Practice-Based PSF

The differences between PSFs and their corporate counterparts emerge clearly when we look at *practice-based* PSFs, where the client is buying the firm's expertise in a particular professional area. By "practice-based," we mean firms whose services are based on *the practice of a codified body of knowledge in solving client problems*. Classic examples of practice-based professional services include public accounting, tax advisory services, strategic consulting, and the law (which is the oldest prototype of practice-based PSFs). Other examples include corporate finance, actuarial consulting, architectural design, strategy consulting, and money management. Each of these professions has a codified body of knowledge that is agreed on but also constantly evolving. In applying their body of knowledge, practice-based firms, such as law firms, use judgment, experience, and, in many cases, creativity to solve client problems.

A strategy consulting firm, for example, succeeds by providing strategic and organizational services tailored to the particular dynamics of the industries it serves. It sells not only professional expertise in strategy and competitive analysis but also judgment in applying that knowledge based on deep experience of clients' industries. It brings to the table expertise that is grounded in both theory and experience. In pure practice-based firms, the true product is the professional service itself. They may also provide tangible products, but those are incidental to, secondary to, or embodiments of the professional service rendered, such as contracts of structured transactions, opinions, reports, and so on. Sometimes products such as actuarial software may be used as tools in helping the firm serve its clients better or as aids in selling its services. Almost never, however, are such products the central offering, as they are, for instance, in software development or in systems integration where the product *is* what the client buys. In chapter 4 we will discuss in detail PSFs that are *not* purely practice-based, such as IT consulting and engineering consulting, where products do figure prominently in client offerings. Although these PSFs are more *product-intensive* than practice-based firms and face somewhat different challenges, they share nearly all of the essential characteristics of practice-based PSFs as described here.

Unlike their corporate counterparts, practice-based firms function as *three-tiered stratified apprenticeships* consisting of junior, mid-level, and senior professionals, as shown in figure 3-1. They are often also organized as professional partnerships even when their legal form is corporate. Junior professionals join firms to learn the trade from more senior professionals.

In a stratified practice-based PSF involving apprenticeship, most learning occurs on the job, working on client problems. This education is sometimes complemented by offline formal training, particularly involving technical skills. But the *important* learning occurs on the job, doing deals, transactions, or working on other client engagements or matters.

Practice-based PSFs are organized into three tiers of professionals based on expertise, as shown in table 3-1. Their organiza-

FIGURE 3-1

Stratified apprenticeship practice-based professional service firm

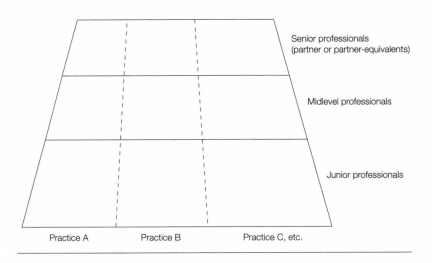

Senior professionals (partner or partner-equivalents)

Midlevel professionals

Junior professionals

Practice A   Practice B   Practice C, etc.

TABLE 3-1

Three-tiered apprenticeships in practice-based professional service firms

	Law	Consulting	Investment banking	Large public accounting firms
Top tier (partner or partner equivalent)	Partner (Sometimes junior or "salary" partners)	Partner, officer or director (Sometimes junior partners)	Managing director	Partner or principal (Sometimes B level or partial equity partners)
Middle tier (mid- and senior-level professional staff)	Senior associate (or solicitor in United Kingdom) Midlevel associate (or assistant solicitor in United Kingdom)	Senior manager or account manager Case or engagement manager	Senior vice president or executive director Vice president (or deal manager)	Senior manager Manager
Bottom tier (junior professional staff)	Junior associates	Associates	Senior associates Junior associates	Senior staff Junior staff

tions are stratified in that status differences between junior staff, midlevel, and senior partner-level professionals are clear and significant. The status differences, for example, between a third-year associate in an investment bank and a vice president or managing director are huge, with managing directors occupying a class of their own. Managing directors in virtually every firm are seen as the equivalent to the partner level. While PSFs are hierarchically flat, the status of managing directors is the same as partner.

The task facing all professionals in the most prestigious firms is to continue to create new concepts and methods that add to and enhance the existing body of knowledge that they use in solving client problems. For this reason, creating new knowledge is one of the most critical challenges facing PSFs. Formulating a new accounting methodology to replace one that has served clients well for twenty years, for instance, demands equal measures of experience, technical depth, and ingenuity; it requires research and carefully calculated risk taking. It also means being prepared to act on new concepts, since they can become stale quickly in volatile times. Innovation and the creation of new ideas, then, is an ongoing process for PSFs and their leaders.

On top of this, firms often exert pressure on their people to create new content or methods in areas in which they may not yet have extensive experience and expertise but where clients have important emerging needs. A new economic trend or marketplace development, for example, may push professionals to create new approaches and solutions—sometimes under severe time and information constraints. For this reason, top PSFs compete for the best and the brightest, professionals who are adept at creating useful practices that might be applied in new ways to serve clients.

Finally, because the nature of their work is typically both knowledge-based and project-oriented, PSFs tend to attract staff who are highly achievement oriented with higher tolerances for ambiguity and greater needs for autonomy and variety than the population as a whole. They are, in many respects "a different breed of cat." They are typically difficult both to manage and to keep challenged, unless the PSF leaders really understand their motivational drivers (a topic we will discuss in detail in chapter 7).

The Corporate Model

The corporate model evolved in the early nineteenth century to manage the size, scale, and complexity created by mass production.[1] The distinguishing structural feature of the corporate model is its emphasis on *specialization by function*, with a clear separation of manufacturing, sales, marketing, and design into differentiated subunits. This specialization and differentiation of roles is what allows large corporations to deal with the multidimensional aspects of designing, producing, selling, and distributing standardized products for mass markets. Indeed, this functional form of organization is still the basic building block or the "deep blueprint" of most modern-day, product-based corporations, regardless of whether organized by function, product division, or strategic business unit (SBU). (See figure 3-2 for the basic functional form of organization.)

Another basic aspect of the corporate model is its *clear separation of managerial roles and producing roles*. When employees progress up the organizational ladder and become managers in the corporate model, they stop functioning as individual contributors. This allows them to devote their time and efforts to planning, directing, and coordinating the work of others. This clear differentiation is essential to managing the size and complexity involved in mass production and mass distribution.

When Jack Welch moved through the ranks of General Electric in the 1970s, he made his mark initially by excelling in his technical/

FIGURE 3-2

Functional form of organization

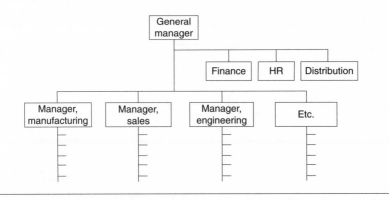

functional area of chemical engineering (in which he had a PhD). At some point, however, he stopped being a specialist and joined the ranks of "management." Welch then began focusing on span of control, working across functions, global expansion, and profit strategies. This clean break from his previous technical/functional role is not the model in a PSF, and it is an obvious point of difference between the two organizational models.

A third salient aspect of the corporate model (and of managerial capitalism) is the *separation of the ownership and management functions*. In the corporate model, managers act on behalf of owners, not *as* owners. The two roles are differentiated even when individual managers are also shareholders. Yet in practice-based professions, the producers, managers, and owners are often the same people.

Finally, in the corporate model, activities are sufficiently routinized and standardized that learning can largely occur in structured venues such as formal training programs, unlike PSFs where learning is done on the job. The essential differences between the corporate model and the classic practice-based PSF are summarized in table 3-2.

TABLE 3-2

Characteristics of practice-based professional service firms compared to the product-based corporate model

	Corporate model	Practice-based PSF
Purpose	• Created to manage size, scale, and complexity of mass production	• Evolved to enable practicing professionals to provide services to clients
Nature of specialization and differentiation of roles	• **Specialization by functions:** Separation of marketing, sales, design, and production functions into specialized departments. These *functional roles* are *highly differentiated* from each other and performed by functional specialists	• **Specialization by practices:** Separation of practices by disciplinary specialties. Functional roles such as business development, client service, and execution are *highly integrated aspects of senior professional roles* and not typically performed by functional specialists
Managerial roles	• **Differentiation of management and individual contributor roles:** Clear separation of managerial and producing roles	• **Integration of management and producer roles:** Extensive use of producer-manager roles at practice-leadership levels and at client-handling partner levels
Staff development	• Learning based principally on *formal training programs*	• Learning based principally on on-the-job *professional apprenticeships*
Governance	• **Corporate form of organization:** Clear separation of ownership and management	• **Partnership types of organization:** Senior professionals typically have an ownership stake and see themselves as partners, sometimes even when the firm is legally a corporation or is publicly traded

Revealing Contrasts

Unlike the corporate model, practice-based PSFs are structured to enable professionals to provide specialized solutions to client problems on a client-by-client basis. As a result, the typical PSF differs from a product-based corporation in several fundamental respects that make an integrated holistic approach to leadership necessary.

Specialization and Differentiation of Roles

Instead of being organized by functional specialties (e.g., sales, production, and engineering), PSFs are organized by practice specialties (e.g., corporate law, intellectual property, etc.) or service lines (e.g., audit, tax advisory, corporate finance, etc.). In fact, business development, client service, and execution (the PSF's functional equivalents of marketing, sales, and production) are *not* highly differentiated roles in different departments as they are in the corporate model. They reside in the firm's senior professionals who handle these different functions as highly integrated aspects of the partner role rather than delegating them to specialists in separate departments. Partner-level professionals are individually responsible for business development, client service, and execution on a client-by-client basis. This is a key reason why an integrated leadership model is effective in the PSF setting.

Even when true functional specialties exist in PSFs, they are typically support groups such as human resources, finance, accounting, technology, and marketing. For instance, when a PSF has a marketing department or a business development group, its major purpose is to assist practice leaders and individual partners in spotting, researching, and developing new business opportunities. It is the partners themselves who are ultimately responsible for business development and actual client contact rather than the firm's marketing specialists, who instead play critical roles in identifying potential opportunities and in enabling line partners to gain entry into new or existing client segments. In terms of leadership, it is the partner-level professionals who provide direction and ensure that the work is executed with commitment. Given the holistic nature of the work, these are activities that cannot be delegated to functional specialists and why an integrative approach to leadership is needed.

Managerial Roles

The melding of producer and manager roles creates unique issues for PSFs. For example, heads of practice groups and office managing partners continue to practice as lawyers, investment bankers, auditors, or consultants in practice-based firms. Also, "producing managers" typically exist at all but the highest levels of very large PSFs such as the global IT consulting firms, the Big Four accounting firms, and large law firms. However, even in these large firms, leaders at the client-service-group level are inevitably producing managers. In this respect, leaders in PSFs are not just providing direction, they are also deeply involved in the execution of client work. They *both* execute and direct others who execute.

The melding of producer and manager roles has always been a differentiating trait of PSFs, but in today's rapidly paced world it becomes a problematic leadership issue as partners find themselves with more tasks than time. In the face of increasing client demands on their time and energy, something has to give. Frequently, what "gives" is their managerial role; they devote more time to producing the work and less time to providing the leadership needed to deal with an increasingly demanding environment. More than ever before an integrated approach to leadership is key.

Integrated leaders recognize that securing commitment is an essential leadership behavior. Despite the pressure for results, they grasp that building commitment is more important to the firm's ability to survive and thrive than ever before. Associates are more prone to leave than in the past. Senior professionals may not bolt, but they often lack the energy and drive that they once had. It is all too easy for people to become disconnected from the firm both emotionally and physically (via travel, more time spent with clients on site, etc.), making it imperative for leaders to focus on securing commitment and providing clear direction.

Governance

The underlying governance model of most practice-based PSFs is rooted in a partnership concept, even when they are legally organized as corporations. For example, Bain & Company, Boston Consulting Group, Booz Allen, and McKinsey & Company, all of which have been legally incorporated for many years, manage themselves as if they were partnerships and refer to their senior-level professionals as "partners," even though their actual titles are vice president, officer, principal, or director. The same is the case for firms like Mercer Human Resource Consulting and A.T. Kearney, even though they are part of larger, publicly traded companies.

Finally, in many practice-based PSFs, practice leaders and partners are also major shareholders, and the clear separation between the management and ownership roles in the corporate model is either absent or at least blurred. When this is the case, the leader's role is much more difficult than in a corporate setting, where the lines of authority are quite clear. For instance, in most law firms, the managing partner's key direct reports (such as heads of major departments, practice group leaders, office managing partners, or star producers) are also among the firm's major owners in terms of partnership units. Managing in situations like this is complex and politically sensitive, often requiring a much greater level of political skill and personal credibility than what is typically required in a corporate setting. Creating a sense of inclusion for professionals at all levels of the firm, for instance, requires that leaders spend more time on this leadership role and exhibit more skill in performing it than in the past. In firms like these, leadership means more than just providing direction (and inspiration); it also means building the kind of commitment that keeps these partnershiplike firms from coming apart.

Staff Development

Practice-based PSFs also differ from the corporate model not only in the importance of staff development but also in how development is accomplished. Again, this is an area that may receive short shrift from leaders producing work for demanding clients. Most learning within firms occurs on the job, using an apprenticeship model that is complemented by offline formal training. Project finance law, for instance, is not learned in law school but in a law firm such as Milbank Tweed Hadley & McCloy or Morgan Lewis. Similarly, strategy consulting is not learned at business school but at a strategy consulting firm. The same is the case with investment banking. *Both teaching and learning occur as part of executing the work for clients.*

An equally important characteristic of PSFs is not only that young professionals learn on the job, but that their apprenticeship is influenced by the firm's philosophy and approach. Because this learning occurs under the supervision and tutelage of more senior professionals, the quality of the teaching, coaching, and mentoring in a PSF is especially critical. It directly affects the quality of work that professionals are able to do in current assignments as well as their readiness to take on more advanced and demanding work in the future. In this way, effective leadership in practice-based firms involves a much greater emphasis on hands-on teaching and mentoring than the corporate model. Not only are leaders providing direction for a practice, they are also running an apprenticeship. Their personal example has a huge impact on what people learn and how they develop.

Integrated leaders understand that what they say and do will determine how well young professionals acquire the explicit and tacit knowledge needed to do the work. They know that if they are diligent, dedicated, and resourceful, associates will emulate these behaviors. And they recognize that if they take the time to communicate information and ideas, they will groom a future generation of PSF leaders who will take development seriously.

We should also note that the young professionals attracted to PSFs often need more "care and feeding" than their counterparts at corporations. As described in chapter 7, PSFs attract individualistic high achievers, people who can be extremely independent and ambitious. Without guidance early in their careers, these individuals can lose their way, picking up work habits and attitudes that diminish their effectiveness. Traditional PSF leaders have always prioritized setting direction and execution, but they have often assigned a lower priority to securing commitment to that direction or to setting a personal example. If leaders expect to develop the new talent coming to their firms, they must provide truly integrated leadership.

We recognize that coaching and mentoring are important in the corporate context, but in a practice-based apprenticeship, the role of on-the-job coaching is critical, not only to the quality of work done for clients but also to the development of human capital. The irony (and tragedy) is that PSFs often do a much poorer job in this area than their corporate counterparts, even though coaching and mentoring are even more critical to their success.

Flat Organizations

Unlike the modern day corporation, the "organizational DNA" of practice-based PSFs goes back to the inns of the courts of London and the Trade and Craft Guilds of Europe.[2] In this regard, the basic structural form of practice-based firms has not changed for hundreds of years. They reflect their roots in relatively flat, apprenticeship-based paradigms. For example, even large PSFs have a limited number of levels between the newest professional and the firm's CEO or managing partner—there are only five levels in a firm as large as Clifford Chance, for instance. They also tend to be what Karl Weick refers to as "loosely coupled organizations."[3] Work is typically done in small teams (or collections of small teams, if the project, matter, or deal is complex) that often spend much of their time at the client's site. These teams are seldom permanent, and with the exception of compliance-based practices (such as audits and certain kinds of actuarial work), teams usually dissolve when the engagement is finished. With each new engagement, new teams are formed based on the types and degree of expertise needed. Their flat structures, the recombinant nature of the teams, and the relative autonomy that partners enjoy in pursuing and executing new work results in a highly fluid and unstructured organization when compared to their corporate counterparts.

Given these characteristics, providing clear direction, ensuring quality execution, and creating commitment are critical leadership activities. This is especially the case at a time when most PSFs have experienced significant growth and are coping with major changes in their business environments. When firms were smaller, leaders were better able to communicate direction, maintain people's focus and energy, and facilitate production of the work. At a time of rapid expansion, however, leaders cannot possibly spend as much time or have as much interpersonal contact with their people. Given the nature of teams within firms as well the autonomy professionals enjoy, leaders must truly provide integrated leadership to keep their professionals on course, committed, and effective.

Importance of Shared Values and Systems

Aware and involved leaders are needed for this flat structure to be effective, but they must also develop a culture of shared values and systems that act to reinforce the norms and values of the firm. When firms fail to do this, they may exhibit a tendency toward un-coordinated—sometimes chaotic—behavior, or a series of individual partner franchises that coexist independently without any overarching purpose. Firms that fail to develop clear cultures and reinforcing systems seldom rise to the top of their professions. In contrast, when partners not only share common values but also mentor and coach well, the firm's culture becomes tightly woven across offices and practices. Partners play a critical role in creating and sustaining this cohesion, direction, and sense of purpose, which is why the personal example they set is so important. Partners who are supportive of other partners in word and deed inspire junior professionals. When partners and other senior professionals reach out and genuinely focus on the career development of their charges, professionals learn their craft faster and become more skilled at creating new intellectual capital, which in turn helps differentiate the firm's practices from other professional service firms.

Some practice-based consulting firms such as McKinsey, Bain, and law firms like Wachtell, Lipton, Rosen & Katz, and Davis Polk & Wardwell obsess over socializing new associates so that the values of these firms emerge in all areas—recruiting practices, social events, written correspondence, training, and so on. Though Bain, Boston Consulting Group, and McKinsey are legally incorporated, and Wachtell and Davis Polk are partnerships, all five are true partnerships in their look, feel, and cultures.

PSFs with these kinds of cultures tend to be faster-paced, more tightly knit, and more intellectually vibrant than their competitors. In the best professional service firms, people feel like they are in the middle of the action and part of a creative, fast-moving enterprise that is on its profession's cutting edge. This is the essence of integrated leadership: the ability of leaders not just to set a strategically sound direction but also to generate excitement about this direction, provide the resources to put this direction into action, and demonstrate by their own behaviors their belief in the vision they've set forth.

The Strengths of the PSF Model

The stratified apprenticeship model continues to characterize successful practice-based PSFs because it is so well suited to the expertise focus of their work, the episodic nature of client needs, and the independent, challenge-seeking professionals that such work attracts. PSFs are organizations in which the key assets are expertise, technical knowledge, and client relationships, and the stratified apprenticeship organization enables PSFs to utilize these assets much more effectively and efficiently than the pure corporate form of organization. This organization allows PSFs to develop needed expertise in their junior professionals while executing client work under the supervision of senior professionals. Their team-based work groups also provide the flexibility needed to assemble, dissolve, and reassemble teams of professionals based on individual client needs. The result is a highly efficient use of the firm's most important asset—its people.

These strengths, however, are dependent on people being motivated and engaged, managed effectively, and remaining with the firm for a sustained period of time. While these factors might have been taken for granted as little as ten years ago, they cannot be taken for granted now. In today's faster moving world, integrated leaders must monitor the attitudes and actions of their young professionals to ensure that these attitudes and actions are aligned with the goals and strategy of the firm and practice.

Challenges of Managing a PSF

The very characteristics of the PSF model that make it so effective for delivering professional services also make PSFs difficult to manage, especially at a time of volatility and unpredictability. The highly independent, high-need-for-achievement personalities who populate PSFs have little tolerance for structure or anything that feels like bureaucracy, and they are usually deeply enmeshed in solving client problems or selling new work. Even on a one-on-one basis, it is often hard to get their attention on issues not directly related to their client work. During times of great change, it is even more difficult to manage these individuals, since partners know that many of their most talented people may bolt if they feel that someone is stepping on their toes.

Moreover, the loosely organized nature of PSF organizations makes both communication and coordination difficult; multiple teams are dispersed throughout the firm and among its clients. As a result, leaders at the practice level face the challenge of maintaining coherent focus. The diffusion of power that is inherent in a context of partnership and producing managers only increases that challenge.

A related danger is that the producing manager role can reinforce a pervasive short-term perspective so that strategic and developmental tasks are ignored or put off. Cumulatively, all these factors make PSFs more difficult to manage than their more highly structured corporate counterparts. It is for all these reasons—loose structures, the diffusion of power, and team-based organizations—that PSFs need leaders skilled at ensuring execution, setting a clear direction, and building strong commitment.

PSF Leader Vulnerabilities

All these challenges are exacerbated by the fact that most leaders in PSFs not only are immersed in client work themselves, but also represent the firm in myriad areas. As a result they too can lose direction. Instead of being integrated leaders, they relegate everything but client work to a back room.

The most common mistake leaders in PSFs make is to lose perspective. Either they are not perceptive observers of their own behavior—how they come across to staff or clients—or they have not learned how to reflect on where they are spending their time. Because they are client driven, they often drop everything when clients call. They become so wrapped up in putting out fires and seizing immediate opportunities that they lack a long-term perspective. In a word, they are almost exclusively focused on execution.

Execution is a central part of the integrated model of leadership, but it is only one part. Exhibiting only one of the four integrated behaviors will result in ineffective leadership. Most leaders at the managing partner level recognize, at least intellectually, that they must maintain both short- and long-term perspectives. The problem of maintaining a long-term view is worse with practice leaders and office managing partners. If they are not particularly reflective about how they're allocating their time, they will gravitate toward the urgent and let the less urgent but more important longer-term issues slide.

Admittedly, this can also be a problem for leaders in traditional corporations, but the action tends to be faster and more furious in a PSF. CEOs and other executives of corporations usually have fewer daily emergencies, are not deeply involved in actual execution, and simply have more time to reflect. The corporate CEO, for instance, seldom gets caught up in the day-to-day work of the corporation and thus has greater distance—or perspective, if you will—to consider the larger picture.

A second vulnerability involves taking relationships for granted. So much of client work is project-oriented and accomplished away from the office that professionals can lose touch with the central core of the firm. This can leave many individuals feeling uncoupled from the firm. For a variety of reasons, which will be described in chapters 8 and 9, professionals need to know they are connected in important ways to the firm. "Connecting" them is part of the work of gaining and maintaining commitment. Leaders in PSFs, like their people, are also often on the road and short on time. As a result they unwittingly take their relationships with their people for granted.

This is an understandable tendency, but one that can be very costly, especially when people interpret a leader's behavior as indifference—and that they, the professionals, don't matter anymore. Under such circumstances people tend to feel marginalized and then begin to act that way; when this happens, they start taking calls from headhunters more seriously. When we are asked to do confidential third-party exit interviews, we find that many times a valuable professional has left because she no longer felt like she mattered to the firm. The person's boss is typically not only surprised by the sudden departure but also clueless as to why. ("She got a great bonus and has had great assignments, and we gave her a great performance review last year.")

Although corporate executives also travel, they generally do so with less frequency and less urgency than professionals. They don't dive into a client problem and forget everything else until it is resolved. Corporate executives are usually close enough—both physically and emotionally—to their people that they are more likely to have (and in many cases value) continuous relationships with key subordinates.

Even more important, leaders in PSFs, especially at the top, often falsely assume that their relationships with other leaders of the firm are solid. In stressful, time-sensitive environments, they may not realize that it has been weeks or even months since they sat down with their colleagues and discussed anything meaningful besides current client problems. In particular, managing partners of practice-based firms must ensure that they make time for the care and feeding of these dynamic but central relationships.

The one commonality underlying all these examples is that leaders in PSFs lose perspective because they don't have clear agendas and don't view leadership as an integrated set of activities that include more than execution. They all have short-term execution goals, but few have simple, focused plans that address strategic issues and the need to build commitment.[4] At year's end, when leaders reflect on what they have accomplished, only two or three major themes will emerge. The challenge for most leaders in PSFs is to focus attention on those areas that are central to the growth and development of the enterprise. Without this awareness, they will be captives of the crises or demands of the moment.

The Problem of Size, Scale, and Complexity

Before we leave the broad topic of how PSFs differ from their corporate counterparts, we need to address the important question of how size, scale, and complexity affect the organization of PSFs. This is a critical question for PSFs as they become large or even global. The newly emerging global mega law firms like Clifford Chance, Linklaters, Skadden, and Freshfields Bruckhaus Deringer are facing and working through many of these challenges for the first time.

As firms grapple with issues of size, scale, and complexity, their leaders may naturally cast a covetous eye at the corporate model. As some firms grow, the corporate model seems to offer a solution to the problems with which they're struggling. As leaders attempt to impose order and accountability on an increasingly large and complex entity, they relish the order and accountability that the corporate model offers. As leaders juggle their producer and manager roles in a frenzied attempt to get everything done, they recognize how the corporate separation of these two roles may increase efficiencies.

For large PSFs, dealing with scale is difficult, because the stratified apprenticeship form of organization is limited in its capacity to manage size and scale. Indeed, the functional form of organization, the building block of the corporate model, was invented by British entrepreneurs to cope with the size, scale, and complexity that resulted from both the mass production and mass markets created by the industrial revolution. The functional form of organization replaced both the apprenticeships of the trades and crafts and the business partnerships that existed prior to the industrial revolution because the old forms could not deal with the challenges of size and complexity.[5] Yet we also know that to be effective on the ground—where professionals serve clients and deliver services— the stratified apprenticeship, led by producing managers, is the most effective structure, especially if the PSF is practice-based.

As a result, PSFs must use aspects of the corporate model to deal with greater scale and complexity without disassembling or negatively affecting the basic structure of the stratified apprenticeship. What this means is that as PSFs become large or global, they have to develop what Michael Tushman and Charles O'Reilly have described as *ambidextrous organizations*.[6] In other words, they have to manage themselves on the ground using most aspects of the stratified apprenticeship model, while simultaneously managing themselves at the firmwide level using aspects of the corporate model.

This ambidextrous organizational model usually involves employing true functional specialists in critical support areas such as

IT, human resources, finance and control, business development, and marketing. These specialists are often better able to get things done than professionals who are responsible for but not expert at these functions. It often also means creating firmwide functions to deal with conflict and cross-border issues within the firm crucial to providing integrated services. Inevitably, increasing size and global reach also means having some professionals who carry little or no client-handling responsibility, that is, professionals who are full-time leaders and managers. This last point may seem heretical, but in large, growing firms, it is necessary to have leaders who focus only on firmwide issues, formulating strategy, and securing greater commitment at all levels of the firm.

All the large global consulting firms, such as Accenture, A.T. Kearney, Booz Allen, and McKinsey, as well as the large accounting firms, have had to deal with this challenge. Even pure practice-based firms like McKinsey, Bain, and Boston Consulting Group have had to come to terms with managing global scale on a firmwide basis while continuing to function locally as a PSF. Managing differently firmwide than on the ground is not easy. Few world-class PSFs are truly global, regardless of profession. There are several reasons why this is so difficult to achieve.

First, as this chapter has shown, the corporate and PSF models are fundamentally different from each other and in many respects are at odds. These differences often result in professionals on the ground viewing *any* functional specialist roles or nonproducing managers at the firmwide level as dangerous bureaucracy, useless overhead, or the intrusions of an alien "corporate" culture. In the extreme case, partners may see the addition of the firmwide functional groups as the "enemy of true professionalism" or as a killer of the firm's sense of partnership. This is especially likely if firmwide leaders make poor business or strategic decisions or are seen by partners as overstepping their authority or betraying their trust.

A second difficulty—and potentially serious problem—is that aspects of the corporatelike structure that are needed at the firmwide level to deal with scale and complexity tend to get replicated at the practice level. Sometimes this makes practice groups more effective because they gain better systems and accountability. In other instances, however, it can create bureaucracy that makes the stratified apprenticeship less effective in meeting client needs. When this occurs, the firm becomes less competitive at both the local and practice group levels. This is why it is so important that a firm's leaders be clear that they are using different organizational forms at the ground level than they are firmwide. It is also why leaders at the firmwide level need to focus on the tension created by these differences, especially early on.

Attending to such tensions is particularly critical during the transition period when a corporatelike layer of specialized functions is introduced firmwide. Our experience is that during this transition (and sometimes later, if the transition has been successful), PSFs are most vulnerable to adding irrelevant bureaucracy that actually impedes professionals' efforts to serve clients well. When this happens, the transition is quickly followed by falling margins, a reduction in the percentage of total number of professionals serving clients, and decreased morale and client satisfaction.

A third problem that often accompanies large-scale PSFs is a sense of being "corporatized." This happens when professionals feel that the firm has lost its identity, or its sense of family or "eliteness." Partners often feel like employees without a voice or cogs in the wheel. Typically, an onslaught of top-down imperatives of standard protocols, revenue targets, leverage targets, and compliance requirements result in partners feeling overwhelmed, disenfranchised, and alienated. A sense of corporatism can occur even when the stratified apprenticeship *has not actually been changed*, in its goals, structure, practices, or operations. Our observation is that when this occurs, the firm's top leadership and its top practice leaders have lost touch with their troops. They have forgotten what life is like on the ground. Worst yet, they have stopped providing inspiration, connection, a sense of inclusion, and the role of listening—the integrated leadership work of building and maintaining commitment. In such cases, it is not increased size or even bureaucracy that is the culprit. It is a failure of leadership at the top and at the senior practice leader levels.

Having a clearly understood strategy, a strong culture, and a set of widely shared values makes *these* dangers less likely and facilitates the transition to an "ambidextrous organization." Having credible, trusted leaders with the authority and powers necessary to manage a large firm also smoothes this transition. In true partnerships, these powers have to be voted on and essentially delegated up. In our experience, doing this is a necessary step in the transition.

Successful firms have dealt effectively with issues of size, scale, and complexity, but they have done so in different ways, depending on their traditions and histories. The Big Four, Booz Allen, and McKinsey, for example, have accomplished the transition from larger to larger with very different styles, as have Morgan Stanley, Goldman Sachs, Clifford Chance, and Skadden. Accomplishing this objective is not easy and usually requires changes to the firm's governance practices, especially if it is a partnership. It also requires strong leadership and communication on an ongoing basis, and *not* just during the transition period. As one seasoned CEO of a large global consulting firm put it, "The need for communicating the big picture—especially to partners—and the need to manage the inevitable tensions between the center and the practices is never-ending. It's the only constant in my job, regardless of the changing nature of the challenges we have to deal with as a firm."[7]

Understanding the fundamental differences between practice-based PSFs and their corporate producing counterparts is essential to PSF leaders, especially as their firms grow and become more global. It is the unique characteristics of practice-based PSFs that make integrated leadership essential. Chapter 4 will focus on the added challenges faced by leaders of product-intensive PSFs.

4

Product-Intensive
Professional Services

Moving from Practice to Product

C hapter 3 described in detail the unique characteristics of professional service firms and the particular challenges they pose. If you are a leader in a PSF, these challenges come with the territory. In identifying these unique features, we focused on practice-based PSFs as the archetype, because they provide the base case—the purest form—of the classic professional service firm. In reality, however, many PSFs are moving away from pure practice-based services toward some combination of product and practice. Although this movement has been taking place for a while in certain types of firms—IT consulting, compensation and benefits consulting, and systems integration have used products extensively in both the services they provide and as integral parts of the solutions they deliver—the product-intensity trend has gathered steam in recent years.

Product intensity is an important variable in assessing a PSF's offerings, because the greater the product intensity, the more the firm will differ from the pure practice-based PSF. In addition to examining this trend, we will also look at the opposite trend—how some product-based firms, such as large systems integrators and small- to medium-sized engineering, IT, and Web-based consulting firms, are moving toward more advisory-based offerings.

These trends raise significant leadership and management challenges for PSFs, as the degree of product intensity in a firm has numerous effects on organization, managerial roles, capital intensity, and training and staff development. We will look at these trends from a few key perspectives. First, let's understand how product intensity is practiced on the ground, and where different firms fall on the product-intensity continuum.

Product Intensity

Product intensity refers to the extent to which a firm's offerings are based on or include actual products. Many PSFs today are to some extent product-intensive in what they offer clients. Indeed, one of the most significant trends of the last twenty years has been the development of products that either aid in serving clients or are part of what the client buys or has installed. An important aspect of this trend has been the packaging or "productizing" of routine or repetitive services in the form of software products. These products can then be used by the firm itself in serving its clients or sold directly to the client in place of the service. Examples of internally used products include knowledge reuse protocols, which enable professionals to access solutions that were developed for previous client problems and standard practice protocols, in which commonly used procedures, calculations, or text are put in standard formats so that professionals don't have to perform them from scratch for each engagement. These protocols save the professional's time, thereby lowering the cost to the client. Nearly all IT consulting firms have scores of such internal products. Even pure practice-based organizations, like law firms, either develop or purchase such products so that professionals don't waste time on highly repetitive or standardized work.

Equally common is when a firm offers such a product directly to a client. In this case, the client purchases the product instead of actual services. Examples include tax compliance software and actuarial software that clients use directly instead of hiring a firm to do the work. Ernst & Young's Ernie was a classic example of a specially designed tax product. Ernie was available to businesses on a subscription basis to deliver online tax advice. Subscribers submitted questions to Ernie, and within two days they had a well-researched answer relating to state and federal tax codes from the most qualified professional within the Ernst & Young network. Here, clients were paying for an Ernst & Young product that allowed them access to the firm's professional resources.

Many firms also develop products as a means of gaining entry to new clients or of consolidating relationships with existing clients. Often, the hope is that the products will generate demand for added services, particularly of higher value-added consulting services. Sometimes, as in certain types of actuarial consulting, the software is actually given to the client for free so that the firm can focus on obtaining more complex, higher margin work. Rapid advances in information technology have accelerated the trend toward productization.

PSFs vary significantly, however, in how product-intensive their offerings are. Take, for example, a Wall Street or City of London law

firm that is largely practice-based and compare it with an IT consulting firm that specializes in systems integration and customer-
resource management package implementation. To sharpen the
differences, compare both of these to a software development firm
on Interstate 495 outside of Boston that works on a contract basis
for a dozen clients, or a biotechnology consulting firm on Lake
Geneva that works for several large pharmaceutical companies developing genetically engineered products. All four of these firms may
be defined as professional service organizations, but what they do and
what they deliver to clients varies significantly in product intensity.
The Wall Street law firm is almost purely practice-based, because
whatever products it offers are embodiments of the firm's expertise,
such as contracts, structured transactions, or documents. The IT consulting firm, on the other hand, is highly product-intensive, both because it develops software products as part of its solutions to client
problems and because much of its consulting involves implementing
IT products and systems. The software developer and the contract
research firm, however, are actually in the business of producing
products; any services rendered are incidental.

The Product-Intensity Continuum

The product intensity of a firm's offerings is critical, because the
more product-intensive a PSF is, the more it has in common with
its product-producing corporate counterparts. Indeed, at the pure
product-producing end of the spectrum, firms like software houses
are much more like the corporate model than the traditional PSF.
This is common sense because the corporate model was invented to
enable companies to deal effectively with the design, manufacture,
handling, and selling of products, as described in the last chapter.

In reality, you can array PSFs on a continuum of how product-intensive versus practice-intensive their services are. Knowing where a PSF falls along this continuum is important, because its product intensity has a significant bearing on what challenges it faces, its key success factors, how it should be organized, and the roles of its leaders. Figure 4-1 describes a product-intensity continuum, with rough approximations of where different types of professional service organizations would land in terms of their offerings. These range from the classic practice-based law firm or strategy consulting firm at one extreme, to a software development firm at the other. Practically speaking, there are few "pure cases" except at those extremes. Most mainstream PSFs are both practice-based and product-intensive to some extent, in that they work from a codified body of knowledge *and* they include actual products in what they offer. Note that outsourcing is not included on this continuum as it is not a professional service. It is the equivalent of running a staff or production function for a client and has none of the characteristics of a PSF. Most outsourced activities are managed as if they were pure production functions, with all the characteristics of the corporate model.

If we look at how different kinds of PSFs fall along this continuum, there are four benchmark positions where many professional services tend to cluster.

Practice-Based Services

Firms of this kind essentially comprise the classic archetype of a professional service firm, as discussed in chapter 3. Their major offering is a professional service that involves applying a codified body of knowledge such as the law, corporate finance, competitive analysis, actuarial science, or the tax code. Often firms that are

FIGURE 4-1

Product intensity of professional services

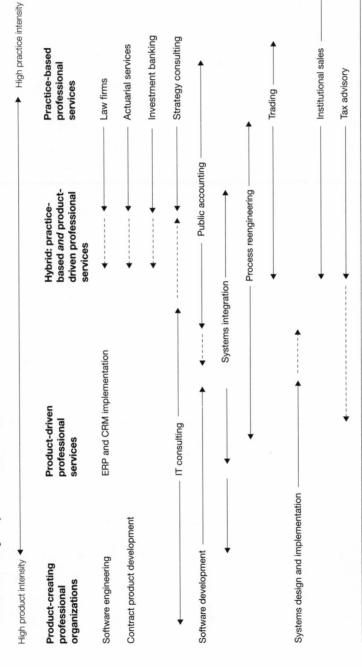

principally practice-based will offer or use some products (as shown in figure 4-1), typically as aids in delivering work or in gaining work, but these products do not comprise the essence of what they offer. Firms that are highly practice-based have *all* of the characteristics and problems described in chapter 3 in their purest form. They are the least like the corporate model.

Product-Driven Services

Product-driven firms also offer professional services, but their services are based on the use of or implementation of one or more products. The classic example of a product-driven service is implementing an enterprise resource package (ERP), such as SAP, PeopleSoft, Oracle or Baan, for a client. The advent of these ERPs in the mid- to late-1990s created an enormous demand for professional services, because corporations did not have the in-house skills or staff to implement these complex systems themselves. IT consulting firms that were big enough to scale up for these huge projects developed large practices implementing one or more of these software suites. In cases like these, *the existence of a product or products—whether developed by the firm or a third party—creates the need for the professional service.* Much of IT consulting falls into this segment. A large part of the implementation aspects of e-consulting, such as Web-site design and Web-enabled customer resource management (CRM), also falls into this category. It is the *client's need for the product that drives the need for the professional service.*

When most of a firm's services are product-driven, as in the case of ERPs or CRMs, the professional service firm is subject to a number of needs and pressures that are different from those in a purely practice-based context. Client demand for product-driven professional services is, by definition, product-based, and products go through life cycles. They mature and become commoditized or demand for them falls, as happened with ERPs and most process reengineering products. As a result, firms that occupy the product-driven space are much more vulnerable to the same life-cycle issues that their product-producing corporate counterparts face, including the need for ongoing new product development of a kind that does not exist in pure, practice-based firms. Similarly, in product-driven services that are technology-based, this kind of product development often involves capital investments of magnitudes not found in practice-based PSFs.

Despite these important differences, however, most product-driven PSFs share most if not all of the characteristics of practice-based firms, including three-tiered apprenticeship organizations, producing manager roles, and all of the challenges related to attracting, developing, and retaining quality professionals. In a sense, their management challenges are more complicated, not simpler, than the classic practice-based PSFs.

Hybrid Professional Firms

A very important location on the product-intensity continuum is the space between product-driven and practice-based firms. Firms operating in this space, which we refer to as hybrid practices, provide a mix of both practice-based and product-driven services. Hybrids have all of the characteristics *and problems* of both practice-based and product-driven services. This space accounts for an increasing number of services, as technology enables the creation of new products and the packaging or "productizing" of existing services. A great deal of the work done by the large international accounting firms and their tax compliance practices occupies this space, as does a significant amount of high-end IT and IT strategy consulting as well as high-end engineering consulting.

Product-Producing Professional Firms

The most product-intensive of all professional organizations are those that exist to provide actual products to clients. In the case of product-producing professional firms, the client contracts to purchase a product that the firm's professionals then create. As shown in figure 4-1, these include software engineering firms, contract research firms, and some systems design firms. Here the professional work that the client pays for is not rendered to the client directly but rather goes into developing a product for which the client has contracted. Some of the work undertaken by IT consulting firms falls into this segment, as for example, when a business hires a firm to develop software for a unique expense tracking system. In this case, the product *is* the product. In fact, in some respects, product-producing professional firms like software developers or the contract research firms described earlier are the opposite of product-driven firms. Whatever follow-on services they offer are secondary to the product and typically limited.

In fact, most authorities on professional service organizations do not consider such product-producing firms to be professional service firms at all. For example, Thomas DeLong and Ashish Nanda's definition of professional service firms explicitly excludes such firms, because they do not deliver a professional service to a client.[1] Similarly, most of the firms that David Maister has written about do not include product-producing professional organizations, except as they exist as part of a larger firm that is in fact a PSF.[2] We include them as part of the continuum for two reasons. First, they define the extreme case of product-intensity that a professional organization can attain.

Second, many PSFs, especially in IT consulting, e-consulting, and engineering consulting, include such operations and products as part of their total portfolio of product and service offerings. This type of firm (or division of a firm) differs the most from an archetypal practice-based firm; in most respects, it is closest to the corporate model, even though it may retain a number of the characteristics of PSFs as described in chapter 3, such as three-tiered promotion based on an apprentice model. Generally speaking, however, pure product-producing firms are organized along the corporate model, with its differentiation of functions and full-time managers.

Where You Are on the Continuum Makes a Difference

Almost all the firms shown in figure 4-1, except the pure product-producing firms, share the basic characteristics that distinguish them from their corporate counterparts. However, they also vary significantly from each other in the degree to which they exhibit these commonalities. Each of the benchmark positions poses different challenges. Generally speaking, the more *product-intensive* the professional services offered by a firm are, the more the organization is subject to the same pressures and dynamics of its product-producing clients, and the more relevant the corporate model becomes.

At the extreme end of the product-intensity continuum, the firms resemble product-producing companies in their structure and managerial roles rather than three-tiered apprenticeships. For example, as a firm's product-intensive offerings increase, its partnership organization with producing managers is likely to be balanced with (or even replaced by) a formalized organization with complex systems and measures, and a greater number of leaders who spend the bulk of their time managing. Similarly, as product intensity expands, so does the need for ongoing product development and the technology to support it, creating a predictable need for more capital investment and R&D.

In addition, most product-driven professional services require a greater degree of standardization and codification of knowledge than do practice-based services, which allows them to develop more extensive protocols for knowledge reuse.[3] Increased standardization and codification also means more formal and efficient training is possible than with the on-the-job apprenticeship model of pure practice-based firms. Figure 4-2 summarizes several basic dimensions (organization, capital, training, management, and codification) along which product intensity influences the nature of a firm's needs. In general, the more practice-based a firm is, the more important the need for integrative leadership for the reasons described in chapters 2 and 3. There are other ways in which product-intensity makes a difference, such as practice segmentation and practice economics, which we will deal with in the next chapter.

FIGURE 4-2

Product intensity of professional services

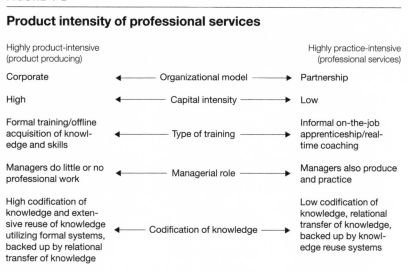

Operating in Multiple Spaces

Many firms operate in more than one space on the continuum outlined in figure 4-1, moving between and among the spaces of product-creating, product-driven, the hybrid of product-driven and practice-driven, and purely practice-based professional services. For example, although Booz Allen and Accenture are quite different firms from each other, both operate along the entire continuum shown in figure 4-1.[4] Many of Accenture's competitors in IT consulting (such as Booz Allen, Navigant, Infosys, Kean, Tata Consultancy Services, and EDS) also operate in several spaces simultaneously, as do the major accounting firms and the large human capital consulting firms, notably Hewitt, Towers Perrin, and Watson Wyatt. Even many small and highly specialized firms have developed practices that cover a significant range.

The challenge for firms operating along the continuum is to manage their different operations in ways that are appropriate for their levels of product intensity. For example, a software development group is likely to be organized, staffed, and managed using the product-producing corporate model: full-time managers, functional differentiation, and fairly formal training or development processes. In contrast, an IT strategy consulting group is likely to be organized as a stratified apprenticeship with leaders who are producer-managers.

A product-driven practice, on the other hand, will have many aspects of the classic stratified apprenticeship but with much more formalized planning, execution, budgeting, and control systems. The challenge of managing various practice groups differently raises questions about practice segmentation and practice economics, and their implications for staffing models and leverage. We will cover these topics in detail in the next chapter.

Migration of Services

Understanding the effects of product-intensity on a firm's systems, organization, and leadership roles is especially important when a firm is migrating from one end of the product-intensity continuum toward the other. Such migration of services can be found in almost all professional services today, but it is most commonly seen among small to midrange IT consulting firms as well as other product-driven services such as e-consulting, engineering consulting, and Web-enabled market research. Typically, these firms are motivated to move to more practice-intensive services (such as those found in the hybrid and advisory spaces) because of their higher margins.

Moving Toward Increased Product Intensity

Whatever direction a firm may want to migrate toward, the basic pattern of what it takes to migrate successfully can be seen most clearly by looking at the IT consulting firms that started life as part of the original Big Eight accounting firms (such as Accenture, Deloitte Consulting, Ernst & Young, KPMG, and PwC Consulting groups). These firms began at the practice-based end of the continuum, where their Big Eight parents then lived, but steadily became more product-intensive over time. Today, Accenture, Deloitte Consulting, and Navigant operate across the entire continuum, although they are strongest in the product-driven and product-producing spaces.

The migration of IT consulting across the spectrum should not be surprising. First, IT consulting is by its nature product-based. The development of new technologies and their implementation by clients created the need for these firms' services, which in turn motivated the development of tailored software and other products. As a result, these firms naturally migrated toward increasingly product-

81

intensive offerings. The second factor driving this migration, as we shall see in the next chapter, is that the large projects with big revenues and volumes operate principally in the product-driven and product-producing spaces.

The challenges that these firms faced—and mastered—included learning how to manage their new product-intensive practices differently than their original practice-based hybrid and advisory services, while also maintaining a one-firm culture. This is no mean feat, as any leader who has tried to accomplish such a transition knows. Another critical challenge these firms mastered was learning how to sell and deliver integrated projects that might include everything from strategic IT consulting to developing special purpose software and systems.

These are not easy challenges. As discussed earlier in this chapter, managing a software development group requires very different skills and resources than managing a group of IT strategy consultants. A quick glance at figure 4-1 shows how different they are. As these firms moved their practices across the product-intensity continuum, they learned how to vary their management of various practices, such as managerial roles, functional specialization, and training and development, depending on where they fell along the continuum, while at the same time developing the capacity to sell and deliver a range of products and services on an integrated basis. These are the two most formidable challenges facing a firm that is changing its product intensity, regardless of its size or the direction of its development.

Moving Toward Increased Practice Intensity

We can see the opposite pattern of migration—from pure product-based offerings toward more practice-based offerings—by looking at the large IT consulting firms that started life as software producers or as systems integrators, such as CapGemini, CSC, and EDS, or as manufacturers, like IBM. All these firms have made major attempts to move their offerings from pure product production to the product-driven and hybrid services spaces. Their desire to migrate in this direction is not surprising. First, although large revenue projects tend to be on the product-intensive end of the continuum, high-margin advisory work tends to be more practice-intensive and hybrid in nature. Thus the incentive for these firms to develop their total offerings in the direction of practice is understandable from both a portfolio and economic perspective.

Second, the migration of product-based firms toward more practice-based advisory services has also had a defensive aspect. Because IT consulting firms operate in the hybrid and advisory spaces, they can often significantly shape the nature and content of the large projects needed to implement their recommendations to clients. These are exactly the kinds of projects that are the bread and butter of large product-based firms like CapGemini, CSC, EDS, and IBM. The danger for firms like these is that the advisory work may be done by a competitor that can also do the large-scale implementation work. This is especially threatening as some firms, such as Accenture, Booz Allen, and Deloitte Consulting, can deliver both strategic and advisory services as well as execute the large projects that often result from their recommendations.

For these reasons, the migration of the large product-based IT firms to include more practice-intensive advisory services has been motivated not just by economic factors but also by a desire to protect their large-scale implementation work. It is not surprising then that all of the major product-based firms—CapGemini, EDS, CSC, and IBM—have acquired IT consulting firms that operated in the more advisory hybrid and product-driven spaces, such as Ernst & Young, A.T. Kearney, and Index Systems, respectively.

Additional Challenges

Now let's turn to the more subtle but no less important challenges that migrating from product-intensive services to advisory services poses. For instance, leaders have to learn how to manage practices that are different from those they started with. This has been especially difficult for firms that started life at the product-producing end of the continuum. A quick review of figures 4-1 and 4-2 shows that the farther you migrate from pure product producing, the less appropriate the corporate model becomes. Yet this is the organizational model that product-producing firms started with and continue to use. We believe that the inability of these firms to manage their acquired advisory services differently from their product-intensive operations is one of the reasons that so many of their IT consulting acquisitions have not been successful. As one IT consultant described the problem: "You can't manage an ex–Ernst & Young or PwC Consulting practice the way you run a software shop, nor can you manage an ex-partner the way you manage an employee. If you do, they leave, and you lose what you paid for."

The second challenge in developing services to cover a broader range is building the skills and integrating mechanisms needed to sell and deliver integrated solutions. This is not easy when acquired firms have very different cultures, premises, and processes that were formed within a different organizational model.

Small and midsized product-based firms attempting to migrate into higher value-added advisory services face the same challenges except on a smaller scale and with less complexity. That's the good news. The bad news is that they typically have fewer resources than the larger firms and are often even less aware of the differences between pure product-based firms and professional service firms. They often also have the problem of how to use an existing sales force that is in the business of selling products as the firm migrates toward offering professional services.

The problem becomes especially salient if a firm recruits partner-level people with PSF experience to develop and manage the new advisory services, which is often the right move. Such partner-level types typically view selling as part of their producing-manager role, which is often interpreted as a threat by the product sales specialists, who see the selling task as theirs. Under these circumstances, it is essential that a working relationship between these two groups be developed and made clear, because predictably there will be both overlap and interdependence in what they need to do to be successful. The firm's leadership also needs to make clear to all key players that a professional service practice has to be managed differently than a product-producing business and why. Yet it is also critical to institute bridging mechanisms so that the two parts of the organization can work in consort when it makes sense. In the early stages, this is not an easy task, and it requires almost constant involvement by top management.

In our experience, the move from producing products to providing professional services is far more difficult than the move from providing professional services to more product-intensive offerings. The consistent inability of systems integrators and manufacturers to integrate their acquisitions of IT consulting firms, as described earlier, certainly supports this view. A major reason for this difficulty is that firms that started out on the product-producing end of the continuum are populated by professionals and leaders who grew up in a corporate form of organization. As a result, either they don't know how a professional service firm differs from the corporate model, or they see the ways in which PSFs are different as being dysfunctional. They are also typically not accustomed to providing the integrative leadership needed by professionals.

In contrast, people who populate practice-based PSFs tend to have a fairly intuitive grasp of the corporate model and are more able to adapt to it as their offerings become more product-intensive. The corporate form of organization is the world in which their corporate clients live, so they come to know it intimately and extensively. Moreover, many were taught the corporate model, especially if they studied business or have MBAs. As a result they find it easier to adapt practices and procedures as their offerings become more product-intensive and learn to manage these practices differently than their purely practice-based services.

Although our experience has been that it is easier for firms to move from practice-based to more product-intensive services, regardless of what part of the continuum you start from, migrating effectively in either direction is never easy. It requires understanding where you started and what that means organizationally, as well as where you are migrating toward and how that needs to be managed and staffed differently than where you started.

In chapter 5, we build on the differences between practice-based and product-based service firms by focusing on how markets for professional services are segmented and what it takes to succeed in different segments.

5

Practice Segmentation

Defining Your Market

The economic travails of the first few years of the new millennium have set the tone for a sea change in PSFs. The dot-com debacle, the telecom bust, and the market crash that followed forced a number of firms to be clearer than they had been about what they were, who they wanted to serve, what they wanted to deliver, and how they would deliver their product or service.

Gray-hair firms were among the most affected by this tough period. As a result of the weakened economy, utilization rates for professionals dropped around the turn of the century because clients were spending less money on advisory services. Bain, Boston Consulting Group, and McKinsey, three of the top-tier strategy consulting firms, all experienced similar downturns in client demand. Yet they also had recently hired many top MBAs with high expectations of "stretch" assignments, many of whom had joined firms without long-term career plans for that firm. To retain their new hires, these firms needed to provide them with challenging assignments, not an easy task at a time when client spending was down.

Joanna McKinnon was a prototype MBA of this period. She had four offers to join consulting firms or investment banks when she graduated near the top of her class. She accepted an offer from a top-tier consulting firm, assuming that she would gain exposure to a number of different industries, functions, and leaders. However, a few days before her graduation on June 7, she received a letter saying that the firm wanted her to delay her start date by six months and begin work on January 1 of the following year. A friend who worked in the firm told her that the utilization rates for professionals had dropped to 50 percent, 10 percent below the 60 percent number the firm needed to make a profit. This friend also complained that the firm had begun to accept more routine assignments from clients, which meant that it had to reduce billing rates to compete with firms that primarily focused on procedures-based practices.

Joanna's friend, who had worked with the firm for two years, was bored and frustrated, because others who had gone to work in more traditional organizations had "real" work to do. Joanna's friend also felt that he was falling behind in his professional development, and he was angry that the firm had not delivered on its promises when it recruited him. Even more troubling, Joanna's friend told her, the firm, like others in its industry, had started laying off professionals who would have been considered assets in "normal" times. As a result of this environment, the firm began saying yes to clients in lower-margin practice segments where it possessed little expertise. The problem, of course, was that young professionals often faced assignments for which they lacked training and experience; and when they mastered the needed skills, they found the work boring and repetitive. Without fresh, challenging projects, they began to surf the Internet and update their résumés. This was how Joanna's friend was spending his time. This was the worst of all worlds for an ambitious young professional.

Wisely, Joanna decided to turn down the consulting firm's offer, suspecting that she too would end up being bored or laid off. Instead Joanna joined an organization that had not experienced the downturn as dramatically and offered her challenging work.

The tough market in the first few years of the twenty-first century resulted in many firms taking on engagements for which their people and resources were poorly suited, and at margins that were not sustainable without changing their business models. As a result, many firms were forced to clarify what practice segments they should focus on. Some firms learned not to promise professionals work experiences that they then could not deliver. They also learned to avoid clients that were not willing to pay for the expertise they had to offer. As a result, many firms have taken a long, hard look at what business they are in, and they are no longer trying to be what they are not. Several lessons have been learned from these trying times. The biggest of these is to know what segments you serve and to align yourself to meet the segments' needs. A second is that you cannot be all things to all people.

One critical way in which professional service firms vary is in the market segments they serve. To succeed, a firm must be clear about what businesses its individual practices are engaged in, which requires a deep understanding of how the markets for professional services are segmented. By asking, "What is the nature of my practice, and what does it take to be effective in its segment?" you can begin to answer this key question. Perhaps an even more important question to ask is which segments you will *not* play in.

PSFs can vary significantly in their focus, practice, product intensity, and markets. David Maister, a keen observer of professional service firms, was the first to describe these differences systematically in his seminal book *Managing the Professional Service Firm*.[1] Based on his comparative research on firms in different professional service industries, Maister identified three different types of projects that PSFs engage in, which vary in their staffs, their leverage (ratio of partners or partner equivalents to staff), and their margins. Maister then described archetypal projects in terms of three different practices: efficiency-based, experience-based, and expertise-based. (See table 5-1 for a summary of the three practice types and their archetypal projects.)

Maister's Spectrum of Practice

By examining these three types of practices in detail, you can determine which most closely resembles your firm or your particular practice. Although the labels alone may immediately identify your market segment, consider the following descriptions as well.

TABLE 5-1

Maister's spectrum of practice

	Efficiency (Procedures)	Experience (Gray hair)	Expertise (Rocket scientist)
Client problem	Efficient solutions to common problems	Customized solutions to generic problems	Unique solutions to unique problems
Application	Skill	Judgment	Creativity/innovation
Critical success factors	• Established systems, methods, and methodologies • Efficient delivery	• Experience • Knowledge • Depth	• Unique analysis • Creativity • State-of-the-art knowledge • Pioneering concepts
Selling proposition	"Faster, better, cheaper"	"We've been there before; we can help you through this"	"Smartest brains around"

Source: compiled from David Maister, *Managing the Professional Service Firm* (New York: Free Press, 1993); chapter 1, from "Balancing the Professional Service Firm," *Sloan Management Review* 24 (1); chapter 2, from "The Three E's of Professional Life," *Journal of Management Consulting* 3 (2): 39–44.

Efficiency-Based Practice

Maister's efficiency-based practice is characterized by what he calls *procedures* projects. Procedures projects involve standardized procedures and methodologies that junior staff use to solve a client problem under the supervision of a senior professional, which makes this method highly efficient. These standardized procedures can be refined and perfected so that younger professionals can excel at doing this routinized work. As a result, these practices offer efficient solutions to common problems. They employ established systems, models, and methodologies, which junior professionals are trained to execute quickly and accurately. These standardized practices enable much of the work to be executed by junior non-partner professionals. The selling point of an efficiency-based firm is that it can perform the service faster, cheaper, and better than its competitors; its delivery must also be consistently reliable. Its success is linked to higher-paid senior professionals leveraging themselves with lower-paid junior staff who do most of the work, which allows a firm to underbid competitors. Successful efficiency practices are typically low margin but very high leverage—meaning that although their profit per engagement may be smaller than practices serving richer segments (e.g., experience and expertise practices), the per-partner earnings are enhanced because much of the work is done by junior professionals at lower cost.[2] Thus, an attractive profit can be made by doing a high volume of this activity while charging less per hour or per engagement than experience or expertise practices charge.

Experience-Based Practice

Maister characterizes the experience-based practice as serving clients that want more than a faster, better, or cheaper solution to a common problem: they're looking for a firm that has depth of experience in solving a particular type of problem. As such clients are seeking judgment and experience, Maister refers to engagements with them as *gray-hair* projects. Because proportionately fewer junior staff can be employed on experience-based gray-hair projects than procedures projects, experience-based firms enjoy less leverage. (The ratio might be one partner to every seven or eight non-partner professionals in consulting, and one to three or four in the law.) Maister points out, however, that successful gray-hair practices are able to claim higher margins, because clients are willing to pay more for the deeper experience they offer.[3]

Expertise-Based Practice

Maister defines the expertise-based practice as one that serves clients facing "frontier" problems—problems that have never been seen before and require novel solutions. Maister calls the archetypal project of such firms a *rocket scientist* or *brains* project.[4] A high level of creativity must be applied to this kind of project, since it involves finding new solutions to typically difficult and complex problems. In attempting to meet this objective, the project team works at the frontier of professional knowledge. Clients go to an expertise-based firm because they are looking for "the smartest people around." Top professionals want to work for expertise-based firms for the excitement of creating new solutions under pressure with other very smart professionals.

The financial margins of expertise-based firms are typically very high, because clients are willing to pay a high price to have their problem or issue resolved. Because of the skill requirements of these tough projects, however, leverage in expertise firms is low. (A typical leverage ratio might be one partner to one or two associates at most.) Partner-level professionals must be intimately involved in the work because of the complexity or difficulty of a client's problem. In the law, Wachtell, Lipton, Rosen & Katz, a top-tier Wall Street firm, is a good example of a rocket scientist practice firm where the partners-to-professionals ratio is seldom more than 1:2 and is often 1:1.

Maister cautions that procedures, gray-hair, and rocket science projects are only points along a spectrum of project types. Firms generally have a mixture of projects that cover a range of the spectrum but seldom all of it, although some very large firms may have a number of different practices that target discrete areas within the spectrum. Table 5-1 summarizes the characteristics of these different types of practices.

Although the world of professional services has changed significantly since Maister described his classic spectrum of types, we are using his three archetypes here because they remain relevant in today's environment. Maister's exhortation that any firm can do good work and make money anywhere along this continuum if it knows where it is and what it takes to be successful there is as true today as when he first wrote about it. In fact, his warning about the tendency toward the maturing or commoditization of practice is particularly relevant today.

What has changed, perhaps, is that no matter how a PSF defines its practice, setting direction, committing to direction, executing, and being a personal example have become crucial to that definition. For instance, an experience-based firm may have been able to succeed in the past without a clearly articulated direction. It could rely on its deep knowledge, experience, and well-honed skills to execute and remain profitable. As competition ramped up and clients became more demanding, however, the status quo was no longer sufficient. Today, firm leaders must be clear on what segment they are serving and provide the direction, develop the commitment, and ensure the execution needed to succeed in that segment.

Know What Practice Segment You Serve

Maister's findings show that a firm can be successful anywhere along the practice continuum as long as it knows what is needed to succeed there.[5] A procedures practice, for example, requires providing cost-effective solutions to common problems with excellent execution in terms of quality and speed. The economic model necessary to be successful in this segment involves high leverage of partners by more junior professionals in order to be price competitive. Such leverage, in turn, requires standardized protocols and methodologies that junior staff can learn to use effectively in creating cost-effective solutions at consistent levels of quality. Serving the procedures segment also requires systems and procedures that enable professionals to deal with common problems quickly, so that they don't waste time "reinventing the wheel." This staffing and economic model is what allows a firm to provide its services "faster, cheaper, better."

Accenture, the IT global consulting firm, is an excellent example of a PSF that has mastered what it takes to succeed in the procedures segment. As a firm, Accenture operates across most of Maister's practice spectrum, but it is especially skilled at standardizing common procedures that it can then train smart, young, junior professionals (hired right out of college) to apply effectively, resulting in very high leverage. In contrast, McKinsey, Bain, and Boston Consulting Group are focused on offering deep industry knowledge and experience, and so belong to the gray-hair rather than the procedures segment. Unlike Accenture, they operate with lower leverage, have fewer standard protocols, and commonly recruit at the graduate school level (typically MBAs) or among people with several years of business experience.

Accenture, McKinsey, Bain, and Boston Consulting Group have all been successful at aligning their staffing and economic practices with their clients' needs. Other firms, however, have gotten into trouble when their economic and staffing models get misaligned with client demands, as occurred with many consulting firms at the turn of the century. Today, we often see this type of misalignment in law firms, accounting firms, and IT and management consulting firms.

Typically such misalignment occurs when a practice group is organized as if it were serving a gray-hair segment when in fact it is competing in a procedures segment. The group is usually characterized by relatively low leverage and highly paid professionals. While this model is appropriate for work in the gray-hair segment, it is the kiss of death if you are competing in the procedures segment. In our experience, misalignment of this sort occurs most often because the firm's service offerings have become commoditized over time. In other words, offerings that clients once considered "gray hair," that is, resulting from valued experience, are now seen as fairly common procedural work. Consequently, these offerings no longer claim the premium they once did.

When this happens, the natural response is to feel underappreciated and complain that clients don't really understand the true value of what they are receiving. A more effective response is to realize that your clients are telling you that your offerings have become commoditized. The way they tell you this is by negotiating significant discounts at the outset of a project or by demanding write-downs at its completion. These are like letters from your client saying that you're not where you think you are on Maister's continuum.

If you find yourself in this situation, you have two choices: either (1) adapt to the segment where you are *actually competing* by increasing your leverage so that you can operate at lower margins; or (2) consciously develop new service offerings and products that will allow you to migrate back into your former, higher margin segment, that is, push yourself back into the segment that fits your current staffing and economic models. From the standpoint of our integrated leadership model, this means that firms must find ways to execute more efficiently or refocus their offerings so that they are more congruent with their staffing model and desired margins.

The worst of all worlds is to continue operating as a gray-hair practice when you are really competing in the procedures segment. Predictably, the economics of your practice will continue to worsen, and you will be killed by smart competitors who *do* know what segment they're serving. Invariably, situations like these are the result of the ongoing pressures toward commoditization of the last decade and a half.

You Can't Be All Things to All Clients

Another lesson that many firms have learned in the last five to ten years is that it is very hard to be all things to all clients. They have come to understand that if they promise their professionals standardized work and then expect them to perform brain surgery, the mismatch of skills and professional challenges results in poor work. Conversely, if they hire very smart professionals, promise "rocket science" work, yet ask them to handle a lot of standardized practices and procedures, they foster anger, resentment, and stress. The challenge, as we have noted, is to create alignment between those hired and the work of the firm, and this is only possible if practice leaders stay focused on their practice segment through both good times and downturns.

Here, setting a clear, consistent direction for the firm can make all the difference. It takes courage for firm leaders to resist a client's entreaties to provide services that are potentially lucrative but at odds with the firm's strengths. Without a clear, strategically sound direction, leaders may find it hard to resist the temptation of being all things to all clients. A set direction, on the other hand, becomes an anchor, preventing the firm from drifting into areas where it does not belong.

A related challenge is not losing your focus as clients become increasingly demanding. Some clients know just enough to be dangerous. They know, for instance, that low barriers to entry often provide them greater choices among service providers. When there are few barriers to prevent others from moving into the consulting space, more firms are created that want to compete on cost. As a result, clients play firms against each other, knowing that margins are coming down due to competition. It is difficult for firm leaders to remain calm and focused about their purpose when more firms are joining the competitive fray and making enticing promises about what can be delivered at relatively low prices. In this highly competitive, cost-conscious environment, the lines blur between efficiency-based, experience-based, and expertise-based firms. Yet the staffing and economic models for each are different.

The challenge that each firm faces is how to answer the following four strategic questions about each of its practices, and then to remain true to their answers:

1. What is the economic equation that will drive this practice?

2. What will differentiate the practice from our competitors?

3. What can we do better than anyone else?

4. What are we *absolutely passionate* about?

What we know is that few firms have the sustained focus to be clear about their answers to these questions—or the resources to compete in all arenas. The exceptions are firms that are large enough to create separate practices with different staffing and pricing models. But even these firms tend to concentrate in only one or two segments, though they may have a small presence in a third. All too often, firms break promises to clients because they don't have the expertise to deliver, or, conversely, their professionals become frustrated or disconnected because they are doing work that is below their capacity. Later in this chapter, we will provide examples of firms that have made clear choices about what segment they believe is best for them in order to serve clients well and meet the expectations of their professionals.

Finally, when PSFs yield to the temptation of being all things to all clients, they create tension among their professionals. The following example illustrates one of the dangers of trying to serve different practice segments. One large consulting firm that we know put together a team of very smart professionals who were seen as the "brain trust" of the firm. To add insult to injury, many of them were hired from other firms and didn't know about the firm's strong culture. This group was called "strategic services." Their purpose was to create the new technical knowledge for other professionals in the firm to use and to be the true strategic thinkers of the firm. In this role, they were supposed to lead other professionals in client assignments and direct work flows, decision making, and problem solving.

Professionals who were not assigned to this "stars" group resented being seen as second-class citizens. They resented their de facto roles as second-tier, nonstrategic professionals. They also resented being paid less than those regarded as "the hot shots." Eventually, the firm redistributed the stars throughout the organization and began developing its own professionals to do this type of work. In this case, creating an elite class of professionals sounded good on paper but became divisive over time, especially given the firm's tight culture. This example highlights one of the challenges of serving different practice segments—a challenge that many PSFs face, and one that must be handled with care.

The Relentless Pressure of Commoditization

Since Maister first described his three archetypes of practices, we have seen an almost relentless commoditization pattern in every major professional service business. This has been the case in every area of consulting, especially in IT, as well as in the law, accounting, tax advisory, actuarial services, engineering consulting, and investment banking. The commoditization pattern is found across all of the major professional services *without exception*. Indeed, the pressures toward commoditization have been so great that they have essentially redefined what the practice segmentation continuum looks like today as compared to when Maister first defined it. A number of intensifying forces are contributing to this relentless movement.

Technology

Without a doubt, technology has been the most powerful factor influencing the commoditization of practices. Firms have used technology extensively to codify and standardize processes and procedures, including knowledge reuse and standard practice protocols. This has driven down costs through efficient delivery of services. Computer applications can accomplish many routine tasks with great efficiency, prompting almost all major firms to adopt new technology to better serve clients. The most widespread use of technology involves computerized protocols designed to communicate knowledge and experience across practices, such as those described in chapter 4. Knowledge sharing and knowledge reuse protocols speed the delivery of services and leverage individual professional effort.

Productization

Closely related to the increased use of information technology in commoditizing professional services is the phenomenon of "productization": the packaging of solutions formerly delivered as professional services in the form of products. As we discussed in chapter 4, productization increases competitiveness between firms, as each one tries to utilize technology to package solutions to generic problems. These products are sold to clients directly or used as the core around which services are delivered. Since such products can be imitated by competitors more easily than high-end, complex solutions, they have resulted in increased competition between firms that attempt to refine and perfect product-based practices.

Transparency Across Firms

As professionals move more readily between firms and as clients increasingly "shop around," it has become more difficult to keep knowledge and products proprietary. In the past, most firms protected their ideas and methodologies effectively. Today, firms have become relatively transparent. When people move between firms or from firms to clients for better opportunities, they carry with them all of their experiences and knowledge, including proprietary information. Technology also contributes to greater transparency, allowing proprietary information to be sent electronically. The liberal use of e-mail contributes to the likelihood that this information will reach competitors. All this has resulted in more rapid commoditization of high-margin offerings than in the past.

For example, one firm creates new intellectual capital and uses the new knowledge with a number of clients. One of the firm's professionals leaves the firm and joins a competitor. The knowledge is now shared throughout the competitor firm, and the two firms

100

begin to create products to implement the new knowledge. Once a product is created, other firms find out about it and put their spin on it. Soon the new model has been commoditized by a firm that differentiates itself by perfecting standardized processes. What was once a novel solution is now in everybody's repertoire. A good example of this dynamic is Wachtell Lipton's creation of the "poison pill," which when first developed was a cutting-edge deterrent to a hostile takeover but would today be considered a commodity.

Client Sophistication and Expectations

Clients' expectations, too, have risen as they try to run their own businesses more efficiently and more successfully than their competitors. In turn, they have increased pressure on professional service firms to justify their costs more than ever. The result has been more competitive "shoot-outs" between firms vying for client business, as well as more client requests for discounted fees. Clients are also increasingly asking different firms for their best ideas or new products, often sharing one firm's ideas with its competitors, including the one they finally choose to do the work.

These four factors have produced greater competition between PSFs and an ongoing commoditization of services in nearly every part of the practice continuum. On the product-intensity/practice continuum in figure 4-1, this commoditization is represented by a "drift to the left." In other words, there is no such thing as standing still on the continuum: a gray-hair- or rocket science-based practice of today will eventually drift to the left and become a procedures-based practice tomorrow.

One consequence of this relentless drift to the left is that the core practice of every professional service industry has been commoditized. The audit and tax compliance practices of the Big Four accounting firms have developed highly simplified, technology-assisted methodologies for doing basic audits and tax compliance work. Even new protocols for testing client processes that were developed by the Big Four accounting firms to comply with the Sarbanes-Oxley Act of 2002 quickly became standardized and routinized and in many instances became the staple of third-tier firms. As a result, much of the routine work that formerly had to be done by CPAs can now be executed more quickly and reliably by trained lay personnel with computer software and technology. The same is true in engineering consulting. Thirty years ago, it took an engineer with a master's degree in design engineering months to do what a person trained on computer-aided design and computer-aided manufacturing (CAD-CAM) technology can do today in a matter of hours or even minutes. Engineering work on CAD-CAM is now routine and executed for less money and at higher quality levels than in pretechnology days. Let us examine in greater detail how these forces have reshaped the segmentation of practices.

Practice Segmentation Today

The relentless drift toward commoditization, together with the actions taken by smart firms in each segment to counteract these forces, has resulted in a significant redefinition of practice segmentation in PSFs. In the midst of this commoditization, smart firms either have tried to maintain their margins (i.e., stay in place) by continually upgrading their services, or have explicitly realigned themselves to adapt to their new, lower-margin segment and then competed aggressively to succeed in it. For example, in Maister's procedures segment—by far the largest segment in terms of total revenues and professionals—the best firms have responded either by defending their position fiercely, or by trying to differentiate themselves in this highly competitive segment by customizing their offerings. In short, smart firms have coped with the drift to the left by adapting to a lower-margin segment, or they have stayed in place by reaching to the right and developing more innovative, value-added services.

The result has been a significant redefinition of practice segmentation in professional services. The extensive procedures segment has now differentiated itself into two large segments, one focused on providing standardized services at low cost, and the other on offering more customized services that are based on standardized platforms. In this respect, the customized segment has taken on some of the differentiation formerly found in Maister's gray-hair segment. Similarly, the former gray-hair segment has taken on many characteristics of the rocket scientist segment, including dealing with more complex, ill-defined problems, firms, or practices, while the former rocket science segment now deals largely in high-stakes, state-of-the-art problems. Figure 5-1 provides a summary of the four practice segments that have evolved over the last ten years.

As firms redefine themselves, integrated leaders must make a consistent and focused effort to set direction. They recognize that as firms fight commoditization through resegmentation, direction can become muddied. As a firm's focus evolves, so too must the direction, from the top down. Leaders must explain both the overt and subtle implications of these segment shifts. They need to communicate the reason behind the shift as well as where the shift will be taking the firm. In doing so, they will enable their professionals to be clear about what might otherwise be a confusing refocus in the firm's direction. Avoiding this confusion—and the resulting alienation and turnover that may result—should be a top priority of leaders.

Most professional services today—accounting, actuarial services, consulting, investment banking, the law, and tax advisory services—can now be segmented into these four broad but different types of practice segments based on the nature of the services offered and their underlying economics. Let us briefly describe each segment.

FIGURE 5-1

Practice segmentation in professional services

Standardized services	Customized services	Expertise-driven services	Rocket science services
Client problem:	**Client problem:**	**Client problem:**	**Client problem:**
Efficient solutions to common problems	Help in making an informed choice from a variety of options and guidance through the process	A major, complex, ill-defined issue of which the client has little or no experience	A major, "bet your company" issue, and the client has never experienced anything like it
Key skill:	**Key skill:**	**Key skill:**	**Key skill:**
Efficient, low-cost delivery of established methodologies, models, and processes	Providing user-friendly advice that reduces anxiety in the selection process and thereafter	Real-time diagnosis and judgment	Providing innovative and novel solutions
Critical success factors:	**Critical success factors:**	**Critical success factors:**	**Critical success factors:**
• Established methodologies, models, and processes • Efficient and low-cost delivery systems • Highly effective training practices	• Established methodologies, models, and processes • Efficient and low-cost delivery systems • Interpersonal/relationship skills • Managing the "sales" costs	• Experience with similar problems • In-depth technical knowledge and/or functional knowledge • Strong relationship skills	• Highest level diagnostic skills • Creativity • State-of-the-art knowledge • Pioneering concepts
Profit drivers:	**Profit drivers:**	**Profit drivers:**	**Profit drivers:**
• High volume • High leverage	• Above-average fees • Good leverage	• High fees • Low leverage	• Premium fees • Very low leverage • May refer work to other providers
Selling proposition:	**Selling proposition:**	**Selling proposition:**	**Selling proposition:**
"Better, faster, cheaper"	"Use us, we'll help you make a better choice and provide you with ongoing support"	"We've seen similar problems before. Trust us, we'll help you with your problems"	"Smartest brains around"

Low differentiation	←——————————→	High differentiation
Multiple providers	←——————————→	Limited providers
Execution	←——————————→	Diagnosis
High leverage	←——————————→	Low leverage
Low margin	←——————————→	High margin

Standardized Services for Efficient Solutions

The standardized services segment involves a straightforward application of codified knowledge to provide efficient solutions for generic problems. As one would expect, the largest percentage of revenues (and staff) in professional services is focused on this segment. Successful practices in this segment utilize well-established methodologies, models, and processes, allowing them to provide efficient and low-cost delivery of their services. They compete with other firms on the basis of the price, efficiency, and reliability of their services. The firms' selling proposition to clients is still that they can do the work "better, faster, and cheaper" than anyone else. As a result, this is the least differentiated segment.

Due to narrow margins, PSFs in this segment struggle with profitability issues—unless they are able to leverage their lower-paid professionals at the junior and mid-levels to perform the majority of the work. Partners have minimal involvement in the actual execution of the work, often stepping into the project only when there is a question or problem, when the deal is being signed, or at other important junctures in the life of the project. Long-term success here requires highly reliable, standardized methodologies and processes, including important *training* processes, since the practice must rely on less experienced professionals to carry out the bulk of the work.

Stephen R. Covey Associates was created in the early 1980s as a way to leverage the number of requests for training derived from Covey's best-selling book, *The Seven Habits of Highly Effective People.*[6] Covey created a training and leadership development firm based on the book's message—the importance of living a principle-centered life. Covey hired and trained presenters in a specific process that would inspire and educate large groups of attendees at programs and conferences. As the program spread, more teachers and instructors were needed to communicate the book's thesis. It is important to note that the message remained the same, as did the process used to teach it.

Covey's firm then created products such as tapes and organizing calendars to leverage and underscore his message, and also opened stores to sell Covey products. In the late 1990s, Covey sold his business to Franklin Associates to create FranklinCovey. Both organizations were classic standardized service organizations. They hired professionals who were mission-driven and trained them to operate with a clear purpose derived from the Covey products and seminars. Professionals who are motivated to "spread the word," or those who are motivated by sales and high volume, seek work at the firm. Professionals who join Covey's firm also want to be associated with a strong brand, deriving the same sense of identity from Covey's philosophy as do employees who work for the Walt Disney Company, Southwest Airlines, or the U.S. Marine Corps.

Most of the large (and many small) IT consulting firms, a number of engineering consulting firms, and some large multinational consulting firms, have a major presence in the large practice segment that includes what is now FranklinCovey. Accenture Consulting, for example, has sophisticated and impressive training for young associates. New hires attend a "boot camp" training process for eight weeks. The goal is to socialize recruits into the Accenture way of serving clients. It is also an attempt to introduce methodologies that transcend geographical boundaries and are used globally. One of the advantages when hiring Accenture for a large IT project is that you know what you're buying, no matter where in the world you buy it. If you are a multinational organization and want organizational change, or if you are introducing a new system worldwide, you don't want rocket scientists tinkering with the process at every locale. You want a consistent, worldwide approach. Many consulting practices that compete in this arena have the scope, scale, and resources to support large projects. Where appropriate, firms that specialize in this segment will work in alliance with expertise-based or rocket-science-type organizations to meet the dynamic needs of the client.

The professionals attracted to firms serving the standardized services segment do not want the intense pressure of always being "on the clock" and having to create new intellectual capital. They often prefer the predictability of consistent processes and products. Many also value being part of a larger enterprise and the possibility of taking on more responsibilities sooner, being able to work without constant feedback, and getting work done in teams. For junior professionals, the benefit of standardized processes is that they can assume execution responsibility more quickly than in other types of PSFs. With appropriate socialization and training, young professionals in these firms can take on more responsibility more quickly because they can master the methodologies that drive the practice sooner.

Some standardized practices may have a leverage ratio (partner to professional) of 1:30. Support, feedback, work flow management, and horizontal communication are critical to success in this segment, because team members must rely on each other to deliver consistent, seamless results at low cost. Firms that succeed in this segment strive to perfect processes at increasingly lower costs. This is the competitive advantage that standardized firms have over expertise-driven ones: expertise professionals aren't interested in doing standardized work, and they can't compete on price for work that can be routinized. As long as clients want precision, consistency, and efficiency, there will be a place for firms that serve this segment.

Customized Services for Tailored Choices

Unlike the standardized services segment, the client in the customized services segment wants more than a straightforward application of practice protocols but is nonetheless still looking for cost-efficient

107

solutions. Tailoring relatively standardized services and products to fit a client's needs becomes the driving force in this segment. While clients' needs may be generic, they want the firm to present them with a variety of options suited to their particular situation and to help them make informed choices about what is best for them. To perform well, a practice competing in this segment must have a broad knowledge base of what options are available, experience in using them to solve client problems, and the ability to see which solution best matches the client's needs. Because solutions are customized, building a trusting relationship with the client and gaining a deep understanding of the client's problem become critical, as is providing user-friendly advice.

As a practical matter, most successful, customized practices also maintain a high level of established methodologies, models, and processes comparable to what is needed to compete in the standardized services segment, because clients are price-sensitive and expect efficient and low-cost delivery. Beyond matching their standardized brethren in these areas, however, practices in the customized services segment must also possess excellent selling and relationship-building skills, as these are critical to developing client rapport and marketing customized solutions. PSFs that succeed in this segment usually position themselves both as advisers and service providers, which enables them to claim added value in their customized offerings.

These firms still leverage junior and midlevel professionals to execute much of the work, but senior involvement is both greater and more crucial than in the standardized services segment. Although midlevel professionals often take on much of the execution responsibility, the customization of offerings requires experienced judgment for choosing what options to present the client, as well as for providing guidance to the client about choosing the best option. A key benefit of a customized focus, of course, is that clients are willing to pay above-standard fees for the customized solutions they are receiving. It is not surprising that many firms that are successful in this large segment also have a major presence in the standard services segment.

Expertise-Driven Solutions for Complex Problems

In the expertise-driven segment problems are complex or ill-defined, and clients often have little or no internal expertise on the topic. As a result, they are looking for help with major issues that go beyond a customized solution to a fairly standard, generic problem. Practices in this segment offer experience with similar problems as well as deep technical and/or specialized knowledge. Real-time diagnostic skills, extensive experience, and judgment are therefore critical for success. Major firms in this segment are investing heavily in knowledge management systems that enable professionals to maximize the value of firm expertise and provide quick access to past studies or colleagues who have previously worked on similar problems. This segment has replaced the gray-hair segment and is largely populated by gray-hair practices that reached to the right as their former offerings drifted toward commoditization.

Successful practices in this segment can charge clients relatively high fees for their services because of the experience and expertise that they offer and the high-stakes nature of the problems they deal with. Providing the judgment, experience, and skill needed to compete in this segment requires intensive involvement of mid- and partner-level professionals, and successful practices are characterized by much lower leverage than practices that compete in either the standardized or customized services segments. Most top-tier Wall Street, City of London, and regional law firms are focused mainly on this version of the gray-hair segment, as are the top investment banks and their smaller but high-end competitors.

In consulting, the Boston Consulting Group (BCG) and Bain are classic examples of firms that compete in the expertise-driven segment. While some of their work might cross over to the rocket science arena—when they create new knowledge and intellectual capital, for instance—much of their practice draws on their substantial expertise and experience. When Bruce Henderson created BCG in the early 1960s, he wanted to differentiate the firm by recruiting the very smartest talent from the top business schools. Over the years, as BCG has grown and confronted normal scale and scope challenges, it has increasingly focused on developing areas of expertise by industry and function. The same holds true for Bain. Both firms have depth of expertise and experience in health care, financial services, and operations.

To take a hypothetical case in this segment, imagine that Harrah's Casinos called Bain with the following four assignments:

- Provide advice on how to centralize recruiting practices for over twenty-five casino sites in North America.

- Help Harrah's human resources chief come up with recommendations to the CEO about how to reduce turnover at certain sites.

- Suggest hiring practices to reduce the number of new employees who leave the company in the first thirty days of employment.

- Help the HR chief institute a new performance appraisal process that takes into consideration different matrices or benchmarks based on job level, location, and time in the organization.

While Bain may have assisted other organizations with recruiting challenges or with a performance appraisal system, the lead partner would not recycle a standard system developed for another client or even one developed for Harrah's in an earlier engagement. While a firm focused on the standardized or customized service segments might rely on a prototype of a performance appraisal system or established performance metrics, an expertise-driven firm would draw on its deep knowledge and skills to make a systemic analysis of Harrah's unique competitive environment, the labor markets it draws from, the types of people it recruits, and how all of this needs to be aligned with Harrah's competitive strategy and its sources of competitive advantage.[7]

A partner from Bain's general practice group or one who had worked in the gaming industry would be assigned to the project. Other partners who have expertise in recruiting, retention, and socialization processes, or in performance metrics and assessment, would work as a team with more junior professionals to create an action-research model of problem identification, data collection, data analysis, recommendation creation, implementation, and evaluation. The work of the firm would take place both on site but also at the office that was assigned the project. What Bain is actually selling here is its deep experience in a variety of industries, as well as its expertise, cumulative wisdom, and judgment in applying this knowledge to solving the client's problem.

Professional service firms that have difficulty competing in the gray-hair segment often experience a vicious cycle of frustration and sub-par performance. These firms are less successful in hiring the best entry-level candidates, so the learning curve for younger professionals tends to be longer and more frustrating. They also tend to be firms where mentoring and coaching roles are not valued, which exacerbates how long it takes for professionals to become effective. These are often firms that take a "sink or swim" or "the cream always rises to the top" approach to professional development, which is viable only if a firm is so top tier that people will join simply for the op-

111

portunity to observe "great partners" in action. But only firms as elite as Cravath in New York and Slaughter and May in London, two highly successful law firms regarded as employing this approach, can get away with it and attract top candidates.

Finally, firms that have difficulty in this segment lose focus faster during tough economic times. They often have imprecise incentive, promotion, compensation, and performance management systems that focus mainly on revenue generation.

In summary, organizational misalignment, violation of expectations, overpromising to clients, and losing strategic focus are all characteristics of expertise-based firms that slowly fall behind. While these may not always be fatal flaws, they contribute to frustration on an ongoing basis. As a result, many end up doing mainly customized services with a bit of gray-hair work. They are seen by other firms as working especially hard for each dollar or euro of revenue they earn.

Rocket-Science Solutions to Cutting-Edge Problems

When clients' futures are riding on the outcome of a particular problem, they are more likely to call PSFs practicing at the cutting edge. The problems faced by such clients, which might contemplate going from public to private or face being taken over, are often beyond the experience and expertise of the people in their company, and the stakes are high enough that they are looking for more than depth of expertise or experience. For this reason, these clients are willing to pay premium fees to PSFs with true rocket science skills. PSFs in this category position themselves as "the smartest talent money can buy" and communicate that "there is no problem that is too daunting." In order to provide innovative solutions, these practices rely on the highest level of diagnostic skills, creativity, and state-of-the-art knowledge; they also demonstrate a willingness to test new and at times risky concepts. For senior members of a practice, these challenges demand even more involvement than in the expertise segment, which is why most rocket science shops have relatively low leverage. This also means that these firms can charge more for their work. Not surprisingly, this segment contains the smallest number of firms or practices.

Rocket science firms' numbers are limited because they must maintain a consistent, state-of-the-art practice, which is an ambitious goal. This goal is thwarted when firms are unable to keep knowledge proprietary. Because technology increases the accessibility of all knowledge and because employees are more mobile than ever before, state-of-the-art approaches quickly become industry practices, and firms lose their competitive edge. As a result, the time period in which rocket science firms can take advantage of and profit from their innovations is shorter than ever. Firms practicing in other segments are hungry to take the innovations of the rocket science practices and quickly convert them into less expensive and more broadly applied solutions.

Examples of professional service firms in the rocket science arena are limited, because relatively few can stake out that ground and stay there. They must bet their enterprise on their professionals, who have to create new knowledge every day; this can be a scary bet. Rocket science firms have no interest in templates or simple models to drive the problem-solving process. If you want to play in this segment, you need to have a particular expertise or niche that sets you apart. The brand is built on a particular set of creative processes and problem-solving practices that, based on the quality of your professionals, only you possess.

Bain & Company founded Bain Capital so that Bain Capital could focus on very complex investment strategies, hiring the very top three or four MBAs from one or two of the best business schools. Bain & Company hired the best students at Princeton or

Wharton to create a stable of very-high-IQ analysts. Wachtell, Lipton, Rosen & Katz epitomizes the classic rocket science approach to practicing law. Wachtell hires only "law review" students from the leading handful of law schools. It promises students that the partner-to-professional ratio will never exceed one partner to two associates. It also makes it clear that partners will work as hard as associates on very complex merger and acquisition deals. The firm has developed a stellar reputation on Wall Street, and if a company is facing a hostile takeover, Wachtell is the firm that will protect it. And charge it. And win.

Associates who join Wachtell know that they will receive immediate feedback on their work, challenging assignments, top compensation, and the chance to become partner faster. The environment at Wachtell is intense and highly cerebral. Smart associates want to be the smartest and most competent in their area. The drive to achieve, to win, and be the best is what Wachtell views as the principal motivator for its associates.

By their very nature, rocket science firms (or rocket science groups within large firms) are not big. They are successful as long as they have a niche, a unique brand that helps them stand out. The challenge for leaders of these types of firms is that professionals can burn out or stress out. Professionals here can be so competitive and driven that they are not aware of the signs of emotional or psychological fatigue. It is difficult to balance private and professionals lives in most PSFs, but in rocket science shops there is often *no* private life. These environments can be difficult for associates who need constant reassurances, because the demanding nature of the work necessitates people entering with a certain amount of self-confidence.

The other challenge is to keep all the professionals feeling included and thriving in an intense, competitive environment. One young associate who left Wachtell after two years stated, "I knew I was smart enough to do the work, but I never felt like I fit the culture, like I was one of the true insiders." As in all segments, there is also the danger that star professionals might break off and begin a new firm of rocket scientists who believe they are truly unique. It is difficult to manage five Albert Einsteins who all think they are the best. For each of these reasons, rocket science is a tough segment to stay in.

It is also important to point out, however, that many firms that start out as rocket science shops work hard to grow out of that segment and into the larger expertise-driven (gray-hair) segment where they can have greater leverage and impact on more companies. For example, the Boston Consulting Group, Monitor Group, and Delta Consulting all began as rocket science shops in consulting, but all actively worked at moving into the larger and higher impact gray-hair segment. The same can be said about Skadden, which started out as a hot M&A boutique law firm, like Wachtell, yet purposefully grew into a large multipractice corporate law firm.

The upside of working at a rocket science firm is that it is intense and exciting. The stakes are always high and clients are often desperate for the firm's help. "Rocket scientists" have the answers, or the confidence that they can create the answers, that will save a client from extinction, economic calamity, or disintegration. Great satisfaction is experienced by those professionals, like those at Wachtell Lipton, who create new knowledge to alleviate great organizational distress.

One consequence of the resegmentation of practice markets that has occurred in the last decade is that there are even fewer rocket science firms in each of the professions than before. They are typically small, specialized boutiques, such as Fred W. Cook in the executive compensation market. What is more common today is the presence of small rocket science shops within the former gray-hair, expertise-driven firms. Most of the more mature rocket science firms evolve into more advisory-focused work. This is not surprising, because such small creative shops in larger firms are sources of new knowledge, products, or other innovations that keep the successful gray-hair-based firms from drifting to the left. Almost all of the classic gray-hair law firms, consulting firms, investment banks, and design firms have at least small pockets of rocket science type professionals who are often catalysts for new ideas as they work with other professionals.

Strategic Implications of New Market Segments

To lead and manage effectively in this new, more highly segmented and competitive marketplace, professional service firms have adopted various strategies, as we discussed earlier. To address the trend toward the left or product-intensive end of the practice spectrum, PSFs have tended either to lower their costs or to add new services. Other firms have responded to new market segments by competing in more than one segment at once. We will close this chapter by discussing these two principal strategies.

Dealing with the Drift to the Left

In the more highly segmented and competitive marketplace, PSFs have adopted two strategies. First, some have lowered their cost structure faster than the declining value of their services. As we noted earlier, Accenture's strategy has taken into account the drift to the left (the natural movement of firms doing more commoditized work). One of its key strengths has been the ability to lower its internal cost structure by routinizing its practice procedures faster than any of its competitors. It also invests a lot of money and time into developing formalized training for every member of the professional staff. Junior professionals can then execute the service with minimal supervision, costing the firm less money per project than competitors. Because it routinizes faster than any of its competitors, Accenture can win business with low bids and still be very profitable. Execution, therefore, is not just a murky goal pushed down to the practice level but a firmwide objective. Leaders must make it their business to support improved execution throughout the firm, and this may mean everything from improved training to improved processes. Only when leaders throw their weight behind this execution imperative will the firm have sufficient impact to deal effectively with the drift to the left.

Firms can also avail themselves of another strategy, whereby they maintain their position on the spectrum by continually creating new value-added services, thus compensating for fast-approaching commoditization and price competition. For example, all the international accounting firms have coped with the commoditization of the basic audit by reengineering the audit process as well as by developing collateral advisory practices in corporate finance, business advisory services, internal audit, due diligence, and other areas. As a result, these accounting firms have opportunities to add greater value and claim higher fees. The firms have also benefited from the Sarbanes-Oxley Act, which has heightened the importance of the audit in most parts of the world and created new, ongoing demand for accounting firm services. This counter drive to the right has allowed these firms to deal with the drift to the left by increasing the value of their services in the marketplace.

Operating in More Than One Segment

Some professional service firms have adopted a different strategy for succeeding in the new, highly segmented and competitive marketplace, and that has been to diversify their practice offerings. When firms compete in more than one practice segment, however, the strategic task becomes more complex. Some firms, like the large international accounting firms, must be able to compete in more than one practice segment simply because of the breadth of their portfolio of services, where they must focus on tax, auditing, and even strategic advising. Such a diversity of practice segments requires managing different practice segments in fresh ways, especially when it comes to staffing models, practice economics, leverage, and margins. New practices need to align their services and resources to a new set of success factors, while at the same time retaining enough articulation with the overall strategy and shared goals of the firm for it to remain a coherent organization. This is not an easy management challenge, which is why no firm, to our knowledge, is a major force in all four practice segments, even though it may have a capability and presence in all.

More typically, firms will have a major presence in one or perhaps two adjacent practice segments and some capabilities in a third segment that supports their ability to deliver in their principal practice segment. For example, as described earlier, most firms that have a major presence in the standardized services segment are also active in the higher-margin customized services segment, because both require efficient and replicable practice platforms. They may also have a capability and a small presence in the low end of the gray-hair segment, which they may need to attain boardroom access in selling large projects. Similarly, many gray-hair firms need to have some capability and presence in the customized or even standardized services segment in order to be able to execute large transactions or projects that involve a lot of standardized work. The actual structuring of the transaction may be in the high-end gray-hair segment, but the execution of it requires some capability to do fairly routine work. Most successful firms, however, focus mainly on one or at most two of the four practice segments, although they may have capabilities and a small presence in other segments. The really successful firms are clear about where they are focused and do not try to be all things to all clients.

Large global firms, such as the Big Four accounting firms, *are* big because they have focused on the largest practice segments. Because of their very size, however, and the ever-present pressure of commoditization, they are almost forced to have capabilities in all four practice segments. This is also the case with the large, successful IT consulting firms, but in neither case are these firms confused about what practice segments are their principal focus.

Maister's observation that good work can be done and money can be made anywhere along the spectrum is still true today.[8] However, with the heightened pressures of technology, changing client demands, and commoditization of services, it is even more important that a firm understand what segments it is practicing in, what it needs to do to acquire competitive advantage, and how to align its organization with the demands of its segments. In the next chapter we will consider issues of strategic positioning and organizational alignment at the firmwide level in order to provide insight on how to lead and manage with these challenges in mind.

6

The Strategic Imperative

*Aligning Business, Talent,
and Organization*

A s the last chapter suggests, thinking strategically about planning is crucial to the long-term viability of professional service firms. How you staff, organize, and price your services depends on where along the practice continuum your firm operates and the critical success factors for succeeding in that segment. All this requires a keen sense of strategic planning and execution, and an ability to think about the business from multiple dimensions. Integrated leadership requires this far-reaching and multilevel vision. Unfortunately, many senior partners have historically preferred to respond to challenges and opportunities as they arise rather than plan for them. As one senior partner in a consulting firm put it, "We haven't spent much time thinking about our strategy . . . We just try to do our best to satisfy our clients' needs. Our practice continues to evolve as we figure out what direction to take."

In fact, some senior partners feel that an attempt to define their firm's strategy explicitly will somehow limit the partners' initiatives and autonomy. The downside of this approach is a reluctance to turn any business away, trying to be all things to all people, and expecting to succeed on all fronts. And even if financial performance isn't as good as the partners expect, they may also be reluctant to exit businesses and practices out of concern for upsetting their fellow partners. As a result, they fly by the seat of their pants. To a certain extent, this reactive, flexible mind-set allows them to move quickly to take advantage of emerging markets and trends. In the old PSF paradigm, this model was fine. In the new paradigm, however, it can create tremendous confusion among professionals. Trying to be all things to all people usually produces a firm with only a vague sense of what it is and what it does best.

On the other hand, when a clear correlation exists between direction, commitment to that direction, and effective execution, it is much easier for a firm to choose what business it wants to be in, define what opportunities to pursue, and determine how it is going to differentiate its services from what its competitors are offering. While entrepreneurial foresight is key, strategic planning's disciplined, analytical process is just as essential in the current environment.

The Need for Strategic Differentiation

PSF leaders usually believe that they understand their business sector and the trends and issues in their particular field better than most. For Jeff Gardner (from chapter 1) and his firm, all the partners would describe the firm's offerings as strategy consulting, organization and change management, and operations management to medium-sized and large companies in the financial services, software, and biotechnology industries. Knowing their markets and areas of expertise, the firm's partners have refused to seek out or accept work involving, for example, systems integration, supply chain management, or human capital consulting. They have also turned down work from companies operating outside their sector expertise.

As important as this understanding of their business is, however, it is usually insufficient. Within a few city blocks of the office where Jeff Gardner's firm is located, there are at least half a dozen other equally prominent firms that try to serve similar clients and provide basically the same services. With an increasing number of "mirror image" firms emerging, the question for Jeff's firm is how to differentiate itself from its competitors. To overcome its powerful rivals, the firm must provide compelling reasons why potential clients should choose its services rather than opt for a competitor. Put another way, the firm must demonstrate how it is different from its rivals in ways that are important to potential clients, by defining its services and articulating specific ways it will deliver unique value to its clients. Creating and communicating this clear point of difference is the only way Jeff's or any other firm can outperform its rivals and do so on a sustained basis.

A clearly defined strategy helps a PSF differentiate itself not only in the client market, but also in the market for future employees. Prospective professionals are highly educated and well informed about opportunities at competing firms, and the competition for them is intense—and getting even tougher. Our colleagues Jay Lorsch and Tom Tierney noted that revenues across the professional service sector increased from $390 billion in 1990 to $911 billion in 2000, and although there was a blip after the dot-com bubble burst, the rapid growth has resumed.[1] As a result, firms have to work even harder to recruit and retain the professionals they need to sustain their growth.[2] It is not unusual for senior partners to comment that the only obstacle to their firm's growth is their inability to recruit the people they want.

A clear sense of direction supported by a clear strategy is an important source of motivation to the high achievers who populate PSFs. These high achievers expect a number of things from their work at a firm: clarity of direction; knowing how their work fits in with larger firm goals; being able to work on complex assignments that increase their capability; and working in a firm whose values and ways of doing things are in line with their own values. In other words, having a clear strategy that delivers a clear point of difference between a firm and its competitors isn't just critical for success in the market for business, it's also critical in the recruitment of the professionals the firm needs to create and sustain that difference.

A professional service firm must start its strategic development process by identifying a distinct strategic position—the market sectors it wants to compete in, and how to differentiate its services from those offered by competitors. As we will discover, answering these questions requires research, reflection, creativity, and discipline.

A Clear Point of Difference

"Which services to provide and how to differentiate ourselves?" is a simple question requiring a complex answer. Although most partners' response to this question is to think about the firm's external market, as differentiation defines itself through delivery, the way the firm "organizes" to execute is integral to its ability to create a clear point of difference between its services and those of its competitors. The way a firm develops the capabilities of its profession-

124

als, for example, or the way it puts its teams together and manages assignments all play a central role in differentiating the organization from others in the same sector.

Answering this simple but key question means making decisions about:

- the type of clients to serve

- the type of services and/or products to offer

- how to differentiate them

- how to ensure that all aspects of the firm's operations are aligned to deliver them

- how to create an economic model that will support the delivery process to generate the necessary profitability

Because these decisions are closely interrelated, they cannot be made in a linear fashion. Since trade-offs are common in each area, PSF leaders must make definitive decisions and avoid uncertainty or ambiguity. In thinking about the nature of competition, let's return to Jeff Gardner's Seattle-based firm. We know, for example, that the firm is in strategy consulting, but who does it currently compete with? Who will it compete with in the future? And for what services? Is it McKinsey, Bain, or Boston Consulting Group? Is it a regional firm that provides similar services to similar clients but only in the Northwest, or a niche firm that only serves clients in the biotechnology industry? Or is it all of these? And what do the companies in these different sectors think of the services of the firm and its competitors? Until this firm is capable of answering these questions in relation to all of its services, it cannot answer the basic question: "Which services do we want to provide, and how do we differentiate ourselves?"

To answer the first part of the question, you must assess what is happening in your markets. Thinking through the following factors is an effective way to do this.

Market Trends

Identifying significant trends and projecting how they might play out is a key task. To begin this analytical process, determine which firms provide the same or similar services to yours; who buys which services from whom; whether they are buying more or less from you or your competitors; and who might purchase your services in the future and at what level. To answer such questions effectively, you need to analyze trended data, preferably over a three-year period, or from the date the service was originally offered, if that was less than three years ago.

A lot of firms are subject to changes in the economic cycle, and in looking at the data, it is important to factor in the performance of the economy over the time period. For example, the major executive search firms, like Heidrick & Struggles and Korn/Ferry International, witness distinctly different demands for their services depending on the state of the economy. During an economic upturn, when companies often expand their range of products and services and/or their geographic base, they need to recruit executives to fill both the new roles and to replace those who have moved on to other companies. Consequently, in a period of economic growth, the search firms are often operating at full capacity.

The opposite is true during an economic downturn. With a reduced number of assignments and a subsequent drop in profitability, it is not unknown for firms to reduce their staff in line with demand. To overcome the negative effects of the economy on their profitability, both Heidrick & Struggles and Korn/Ferry have broadened the scope of their activities by offering related services like executive coaching, executive assessment, and advice on corporate governance, targeted at the same executive population as their core business. While these services could experience similar fluctuations in demand, both firms believe that since the services are targeted at improving the capability of the executives, whose recruitment they facilitate, and thus the boards that a lot of these executives sit on, they will be much less demand-sensitive.

In addition to broadening its service offerings targeted at its core market, Korn/Ferry also started a search business, Futurestep, targeted at midlevel executives. Taking advantage of technology, this service is heavily Web-enabled and uses less consultant time in the search process, enabling Korn/Ferry to price the service at a reduced rate to its executive search business. By charging at a lower rate for this new service, Korn/Ferry has been able to develop a new market, with significantly higher volumes and less market sensitivity than its core executive search business, attracting new clients in addition to extending the services it provides to existing clients.

The question about which companies buy which services from whom ignores a critical factor, however: the possibility that the firms currently competing with each other will be joined by other firms, thus expanding and intensifying the competitive climate. The more technology-enabled search business didn't just expand the service offering of Korn/Ferry; it also resulted in the emergence of a number of new competitors, the most well-known of which is monster.com. Without the costs associated with highly knowledgeable industry consultants and strong client relationships, which have been built on the back of many successful executive search assignments, firms like monster.com were able to take advantage of the lower barriers to entry and, through effective marketing, to create a strong position in the market.

Understanding who you might compete with in the future is especially important, and the convergence of many sectors makes it even more so. In general, PSFs, unlike their product-producing counterparts, have fewer barriers to entry. Start-up costs are lower since there is no need for manufacturing facilities, inventory, and so on. Similarly, the extreme mobility of professionals makes it relatively easy for a deep-pockets firm to hire the talent it needs to hit the ground running. Even without the intervention of a deep-pockets firm, the general mobility of professionals usually brings with it the potential for service replication and enhanced competition, which typically means increased speed of margin erosion. Understanding potential changes in the dynamics of your markets is critical, as strategies based on a static competitive arena can be fatally flawed.

For some firms, changes in the regulatory environment can also impact market dynamics. In the late 1990s, the U.S. Securities and Exchange Commission (SEC) expressed major concerns about the auditing systems and processes of accounting firms, which their consulting businesses had installed. The SEC's concerns had a significant impact in particular on the (then) Big Five, with the likes of PricewaterhouseCoopers and Ernst & Young opting to sell their consulting businesses in order to retain the perception of independence critical in the fulfillment of the attest function. The introduction of the Sarbanes-Oxley Act, following the collapse of Enron and the other corporate scandals of the late 1990s and early 2000, also had a distinct impact on the auditing profession. From experiencing a slow but steady decline in audit fees, the renewed importance of corporate governance and internal controls renewed the importance of the audit. As a result, the trend toward lower fees has been reversed, with audit firms increasing their fees in line with the increased importance of the attest function. Although not all PSFs are directly affected by regulatory changes, devoting time and energy to analyzing the implications of regulatory shifts can help develop a more effective strategy.

Market Readiness

More than one PSF has fallen in love with a new service only to discover ex post facto that the service was launched before clients were willing to pay for it or that the service was more appealing in theory than practice. Both Heidrick & Struggles and Korn/Ferry successfully expanded their service offerings in the area of executive search, creating new markets for their services. But not all firms have judged the market's readiness for their services as accurately.

A number of firms, for example, assumed that e-learning would become the central learning delivery channel in the future. Unfortunately, most of these firms neglected to consider whether the people they expected to lead the e-learning revolution (the Gen Xers and Gen Yers) would want to learn solely in front of a screen. And in fact, they didn't. While they were satisfied spending their nonwork time doing what they wanted on their computers, they did not want to learn their jobs through this single medium. In particular, they indicated that they missed the social element of the learning process. While e-learning certainly has its place and may become more viable as the technology advances, some PSFs invested heavily in e-learning content or portals, only to find that the demand for this service was far lower than expected.

Service Necessity

During strategy development, PSF leaders should consider what services they *must* offer versus those that are optional. While it is crucial to evaluate service offerings based on market expectations and acceptability, what their competitors are doing, and the forecast profitability of their services, PSFs often find themselves with another issue to consider. Many times, certain services must be offered regardless of whether competitors have superior services or the forecast profitability is low. In human resources (HR) consulting, for example, professionals with expertise in human capital consulting are in short supply, and some firms have much stronger human capital practices than others. But if you are an HR consulting firm, the question is whether you can afford *not* to offer human capital consulting as one of your service lines. If you don't, you risk being viewed as incomplete by clients, who see human capital consulting as the umbrella under which other services are developed and delivered.

Service Profitability and Cost Structure

Understanding how much money you make from each of your services (and from whom) is crucial. While much of a PSF's cost structure is essentially fixed, ask whether changes in demand make the service more or less profitable, or whether demand cost, and therefore profitability, is neutral. Understanding the impact of any changes on the cost structure of your existing service offering and service delivery process is key, as is estimating the likely cost and profitability of any new services. Not all firms know the answer to these questions, and in less competitive markets not knowing the answers was not detrimental. Today, however, failing to assess these issues can prove costly—especially when firms front-load the cost structure without an accurate understanding of the likely demand for the service. Intellinex (now ACS), initially established by Ernst & Young as its wholly owned e-learning subsidiary, did exactly that in 2000, recruiting heavily in anticipation of a demand that didn't materialize and having to lay off people that it had only just recruited.[3]

Which Services and How to Differentiate Them

The data generated from the analysis discussed should provide a clear indication of which services to focus on. The next task is to determine how your services are perceived in relation to those of your competitors. Market share data can provide some indication, but it rarely provides the whole truth. For example, some firms may be buying share and thus skewing the share and profitability figures. Having deduced what you can from the available data, the next step in answering the differentiation question is to ask prospective purchasers why they choose specific suppliers. Sometimes this can be a sobering exercise, but the answers can be invaluable.

Once you know how your firm's services are perceived relative to those of your competitors, start to formulate a clear point of difference. An examination of a classic, highly illustrative example from the world of strategy consulting may help. McKinsey pioneered consulting for the top management of major corporations on strategy and broad, general management issues. It aggressively exploited its first-mover advantage and established itself as the premier consulting firm through the 1960s. McKinsey's traditional approach was to build strong relationships with its clients through a network of offices located in major cities in the United States and Europe. The firm's philosophy was to consider every client problem as unique, and it steadfastly resisted developing standard analytical frameworks or methodologies for fear that its analysis might become constrained by the use of such tools. Its team of highly intelligent, well-trained, and experienced consultants would deeply immerse themselves in the client's problems and customize specific recommendations for a particular client.

In the mid-1960s, Bruce Henderson, the founder of Boston Consulting Group challenged McKinsey's dominance in strategy consulting and established his fledgling firm on the basis of "thought leadership"—leading analytical concepts that had general applications. Using simple, powerful, and novel concepts like the experience curve and growth share matrix, BCG quickly made major inroads into strategy consulting. Its rigorous analytical approach appealed to a growing segment of clients that had become increasingly sophisticated and dissatisfied with McKinsey's more general approach. Though targeting many of the same clients and working on similar issues as McKinsey, BCG offered a new approach and delivered it in a decidedly different manner. Through its emphasis on thought leadership, BCG initially positioned itself in the rocket science segment. (See chapter 5 for a complete discussion of all market segments.) However, it gradually migrated to the expertise-driven segment because the volume of work there was far larger. In moving, BCG entered the very segment that McKinsey had dominated for decades, but it was able to continue to differentiate itself from its rival through its emphasis on the use of proprietary analytical concepts.

In the early 1970s, Bill Bain, a partner at Boston Consulting Group, and a few select colleagues formed Bain & Company. The firm sought to target the same type of clients, offering advice on strategy and general management, but its approach was quite different. In fact, Bain & Company created two key differentiators. The first was client exclusivity (it only served one client in a given industry), and the second was a focus on implementation. Bain consultants worked closely with their clients both in developing recommendations and in turning the recommendations into action. This emphasis on client exclusivity (and the close relationship it created with the clients) and implementation was very appealing to some of the major companies that had become increasingly frustrated with consultants who would make recommendations, but leave what they saw as the difficult part, the implementation, to the client.

To a casual observer, McKinsey, BCG, and Bain may appear to have served the same type of clients and provided essentially the same type of services, but critical differences existed in their service offerings. Each firm established a position that appealed to a targeted group of clients. Some clients preferred a strong analytical orientation, some placed a premium on close relationships and implementation, while others valued a more general approach based on deep expertise and extensive experience. Thanks to their clear positioning, the three firms were able to establish their respective uniqueness in the marketplace.

The Integrated Leadership Model

Although some of the early differentiators between McKinsey, BCG, and Bain are no longer as distinct, all three firms remain at the top of the strategy consulting league with reputations for outstanding work. One of the well-known quotes you often hear from chief executives is, "No one ever got fired for hiring McKinsey," and the same can be said of both Bain and BCG. So how have these three firms with long histories managed to sustain their initial reputations and remain the firms of choice in strategy consulting?

Though the firms are not consciously aware of the integrated leadership model, they employ the principles of the model. Each differentiates itself through delivery of outstanding work, and this ability is made possible because their leaders set a clear direction, secure commitment from their professionals to that direction, execute that direction with skill and speed, and set personal examples that reinforce that direction. It is easy to miss that these principles are the key to their success, since everyone focuses on how they deliver outstanding work. McKinsey, BCG, and Bain sustained their reputations by achieving the following: having the right profession-als with the right delivery capabilities; establishing a structure and processes that supported the firm's obsessive commitment to exe-cution; and creating an overarching culture committed to ensuring that everything they do is about staying at the forefront of all as-pects of service delivery.

Coordinating overarching leadership behaviors enables firms to meet these ambitious goals. For instance, when leaders establish a clear direction and secure commitment to it, talent management becomes a much easier process. Everyone in the firm knows the type of professionals they need to hire to execute the stated direc-tion, and new hires are clear about what this direction involves. More specifically, integrated leadership helps the talent manage-ment process achieve the following objectives:

- Access and hire the professionals the firm needs to execute its strategy.

- Ensure that new hires are quickly integrated into the firm's culture and become as obsessive about the firm and what it stands for as everyone else.

- Make sure that the most talented professionals are stretched, challenged, motivated, and stay in the firm.

- Ensure that the professionals develop their capabilities faster and more effectively than the firm's competitors (which we call "speed to experience").

- Make sure the firm has the necessary bench strength to compete successfully on a sustained basis.

- Have a simple, systematic way of reviewing talent across the firm, which enables the firm to match professionals with market opportunities.

- Provide the firm leaders with a view of who the top professionals in the firm are and how they are performing—especially those on partner track.

Of course, talent management doesn't exist in a vacuum. Integration or alignment of different processes is a continuous challenge. Firm leaders, for instance, must align the talent management process with the process of securing business. Winning business without having the professionals to deliver it in line with, or beyond, the client's expectations will have a negative impact on the firm's reputation; employing a group of high achievers who don't receive the opportunity to interpret the profession's body of knowledge and serve clients will also have negative consequences. Alignment, therefore, must become an imperative for PSF leaders today. The following case history will demonstrate how integrated leaders achieve alignment between business and talent strategies, and how performance gains are the result.

Herbert Smith's Real Estate Practice

Herbert Smith is one of the world's leading international law firms. Headquartered in London, the firm has a network of eleven hundred lawyers across Europe and Asia. The firm's major practice areas include dispute resolution, corporate, finance, European Union and competition, employment, intellectual property, and real estate. With profit per equity partner at £839,000 ($1.6 million), the firm is the third most successful of those headquartered in the United Kingdom, based on profit per professional. The firm's partners believe that much of the firm's success is built on its technical excellence and distinctive culture. Predicated on recruiting some of the most talented professionals in the market, the partners feel that the combination of technical expertise with individuality and collegiality makes the firm distinctly different from most of its competitors. The combination of individuality and collegiality is evidenced in many different ways, including the way the firm is led. Despite the firm's size, for example, it is lightly managed, and any notion of "corporatization" is anathema to its partners.

The reputation of the real estate practice, recognized by its recent awards as "Real Estate Team of the Year 2006" by *The Lawyer* and "Property Team of the Year 2006" by *Legal Week*, generates a particular sense of achievement and pride in the practice's partners. Only seven years ago, the practice was underperforming compared to the rest of the firm, and its partners worried that they were holding back their colleagues' earnings. Despite being net consumers rather than contributors, the real estate partners felt that they had the potential to become a major player in the property market. This was especially true of the group of younger partners, who had been promoted in the mid- to late nineties, and of Iain Rothnie, who was one of the group of younger partners and appointed to head the department in 2000. These moves enabled the group to initiate a review of the practice's activities.

At the time, the practice was often subject to explicit criticism in the monthly management committee meetings. This criticism, along with the partners' sense that their colleagues in other practices wondered what they were doing to address their underperformance, had led to something of a bunker mentality. The partners reduced their participation in firmwide activities like training programs, seminars, or committee meetings, focusing all of their effort on improving the performance of the practice. This included reducing their trainee intake from twenty-one to twelve as part of a reduction in the cost base of the practice. But the feeling of being "looked at" also had positive results. The partners became close friends, often socializing with each other, and shared a determination to turn the practice around.

The firm's review of the real estate practice, which took place in the spring of 2000, was set against the backdrop of a rapidly changing marketplace, with much of the work the real estate practice had historically relied on, particularly at the commoditized end of the market, under threat from a variety of sources able to offer lower prices. The review also suggested that the real estate practice had undersold its potential to be at the forefront of the changes in the market, particularly given the corporate, finance, and tax expertise at its disposal in the firm.

At an offsite meeting, the real estate partners accepted that they had to reorient their activities and seek high-value premium work from premium clients. What that meant was debated at length: What type of work? For which clients? How to persuade them to buy? How to manage the clients the firm no longer wants? And critically, how to develop the capabilities to deliver the work? At the end, despite some disagreements, the partners were all clear about what they had to do. While some clients provided the higher-value work the practice was targeting, many did not. The partners identified which clients did and which did not. For those that did not, they tried to determine if they would in the future. The partners also targeted companies that would provide the high-value work they sought and put in place specific plans to develop relationships with the key people in each company. They also had to manage the client tail—those clients on which in reality the practice only broke even or lost money.

They also addressed delivery questions: How were they going to enhance everyone's capability, including their own? How should they make sure they recruited and retained the talent they needed? Was there a better way to organize? And how did they ensure that everyone knew how they were doing and stayed focused?

At the time, all the firm's trainees rotated through each practice before qualifying in one of them. For some trainees, the lure of dispute resolution or corporate enticed them away from the real estate practice, but for others, the early opportunity to run their own files, and greater exposure to the practice's clients, provided the kind of immediate feedback that personalities with a high need for achievement crave. So, despite being far from the leading practice in the firm, the practice leaders succeeded in persuading some of the most talented trainees to join them. Keeping up the flow of highly talented professionals was integral to the future success of the practice, and the partners knew that any changes to the way the practice operated must not restrict this flow. In fact, rather than restructuring along more traditional, specialist lines from their current practicewide approach, the review posed a different question: what fee-earning resource is necessary to deliver the work of the required standard and at the highest profitability level?

The answer to that question gave rise to a radically different solution than had been expected—the concept of *layering*. With this approach, the real estate practice introduced a structured education program for all young associates, which gave them the necessary building blocks of commercial property law. With these basics in place, the partners identified the areas of work they considered should be undertaken by the associates in the next two years to enable them to develop a broad platform from which they could move on to more complex and specialized work. The partners also accepted that the increasing complexity in the market meant that some of them, together with a number of senior associates, would need to specialize. Critically, the human capital allocation process was restructured to take into account the development needs of all the practice's associates.

One of the realities within the firm at the time was an unwillingness to be honest with the associates about their performance. The real estate practice leaders recognized that this had to change, and they began being frank with associates and managing their careers and expectations more explicitly. They prioritized the partner pipeline and communicated clearly with the senior associates about their place in the rankings. Promotion was no longer based on seniority, but on capability, contribution, and readiness. They also decided, contrary to the firm's norms, that there were some senior associates who were integral to delivering the work, and thus, although they would never be partners, would remain in the practice.

While these actions could be initiated within the practice, a number of firmwide activities were launched that also supported changes in the real estate practice. The first were development centers for associates and senior associates. These centers provided each participant a personalized development plan containing both the legal and nonlegal learning necessary for progressing through the practice. With each associate's development now clear to both the individual and the partners, the process of allocating associates to files could be even more focused, enabling the associate's development needs to be addressed faster and more efficiently. The second initiative was targeted at the partners. Conscious that most of the partners in the firm rarely received any feedback on their own performance, the head of HR introduced a 360-degree appraisal process that provided each partner with personal feedback from their peers and subordinates. The feedback was driven by an explicit model of what was expected of a partner—something that before had always been implicit.

Finally, the review suggested one other key change: the partners must run the practice as a business. The lack of financial management was highlighted in the review, and from day one the intention was to expose the partners both to their own and to their colleagues' key financial operating data. For the first time, each partner's work-in-progress weeks, billing rates, utilization, recovery rates, and discounts were to be published and discussed as part of driving the change from being a traditional legal practice to being a legal business.

As noted earlier, the Herbert Smith real estate practice won two awards in 2006, as the real estate and property team of the year, and its increase in financial performance mirrors its success in the external market. Its fee income has risen 50 percent, from £16 million ($31 million) to £24.6 million ($47.6 million) with no change in head count, while expenses have only increased by 25 percent (see figure 6-1). This improved financial performance can be attributed to many factors, including the firm restructuring from a traditional legal practice to a business more in tune with the needs of the market.

In addition, the restructuring also had a positive impact on associates, who saw the benefits of having a structured development plan and the ability to gain experience in a number of disciplines. The culture, too, reflected a renewed commitment to execution. Perhaps most important, everyone was encouraged to talk about how to do things better. At the same time, everyone expressed a

FIGURE 6-1

Fee income and expenses, Herbert Smith real estate practice, 1997–2006

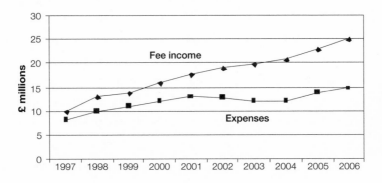

Source: Herbert Smith internal document. Used with permission.

tremendous amount of respect for each other. They had some big disagreements, but when they decided what to do, they marched together. In other words, the partnership ethos came through strongly: "We will help each other out even if our personal billings are impacted."

Aligning Business, Organization, and Talent

As the example of the Herbert Smith real estate practice illustrates, financial performance can improve significantly when a firm or a practice aligns all its internal structures, processes, and activities— its "organization" as a whole—with its strategy. Organizational alignment has its roots in the work of Paul Lawrence and Jay Lorsch, both professors at the Harvard Business School, who found that high-performing companies in different industries developed organizations and procedures that were uniquely adapted to the particular demands posed by their industry segments.[4]

In their now-classic study, they demonstrated empirically that there was no single "right way" to organize, and that high-performing firms in one industry segment were organized quite differently from high performers in other industry segments. Their work led to the development of contingency theory, which is based on the premise that a firm's organization should be fitted to executing those activities that are critical to its success, given its unique strategy and the demands of its business environment. The more aligned a firm is with its strategic positioning, the more effectively it will execute its strategy, and the better it will perform in its markets and financially.

The concept of alignment dovetails with our integrated leadership model, which is predicated on the belief that by integrating leadership activities, the leaders of a firm or practice will increase its performance. Let us return to the Herbert Smith example as a way of looking at the four elements of the model and how they facilitate performance-enhancing alignment.

Direction

Being explicit about the firm's direction and goals is important in any organization, but it is critical in a PSF. Professionals want to know how their work fits into the bigger picture. By providing clarity in direction, firm leaders ensure the firm's professionals are focused on the same target and understand their role in getting there. The four activities involved in setting direction are:

- Establishing goals

- Communicating strategy

- Setting objectives and measures

- Enhancing your group's reputation

One of the problems facing the Herbert Smith real estate practice in 2000 was that it had no sense of direction around which the partners or associates could unite. The change in market focus to "premium work from premium clients" and all that that entailed provided a coalescing point for all the partners and associates. Goals were set for the practice as a whole and for the individual partners and their teams. Performance data was shared, initially between the partners, and then as well with the associates, who for the first time were aware of how the practice was performing. "Opening the books" also acted as a motivational tool, as the associates felt much more closely involved with what the practice was trying to achieve and what their role was in achieving it. The fact that the sense of direction had been developed following a rigorous analysis of the marketplace made it even more compelling to the professionals in the practice.

Gaining Commitment

Professionals have an innate need to be involved and included. When they feel excluded, they feel alienated and fail to focus on the task at hand. When professionals are committed, they work smarter and more creatively to ensure that their project, the practice, or the firm is moving in the right direction. The activities required of leaders to gain the commitment of their professionals are:

- Inspiring people

- Building trust

- Embedding values

- Recognizing the right behavior

Herbert Smith was a very traditional law firm in its early years, so when partners decided to share performance data in 2002, it helped associates feel that they were a part of the solution. This feeling was enhanced when the partners relinquished more power and responsibility to their senior associates, who, in turn passed it on to the associates. As a result of being included, associates were more committed to the firm's direction.

Honest feedback also bolstered this commitment. As the next chapter will show, talented professionals with a high need for achievement require this feedback for their growth and development. Although the feedback was harsh at times, it also demonstrated to associates that partners cared about helping them grow in their jobs. They reciprocated by working with a renewed sense of purpose. Partners also gave associates unprecedented access to strategic information and solicited their ideas about strategy and direction. This secured commitment not only to the firm but also to the firm's direction. This is an important distinction from an alignment standpoint. Associates were not simply swearing loyalty to a general notion of what the firm stood for, but to the specific strategy it needed to implement.

Execution

With differentiation a function of delivery, execution is the key. Truly effective execution only occurs when a firm has clarity in its direction and professionals with the right levels of capability committed to delivering client value. To ensure their firm is able to differentiate itself from its competitors, firm leaders must carry out the following activities:

- Building and delivering client value

- Building the right teams

- Developing your people

- Managing the numbers

Instead of opting for a traditional PSF solution for building and delivering client value, the real estate partners turned the question on its head and asked what level of expertise was needed to do this type of work. The practice placed associates on small teams with one or two partners, helping them gain the necessary technical knowledge, manage more sophisticated client relationships, and bring in business much faster than in the past. Ensuring that the associates were allocated to files that stretched their capabilities also increased the associates' "speed to experience," which helped associates become ready to take on increasingly complex assignments more quickly and effectively than associates in competitor firms. Along with the increase in speed to experience came improvements in client service and client value. As a result, not only did the practice's profitability increase dramatically, but its reputation for moving associates into key engagement roles with great speed helped the practice recruit internally.

Personal Example

Partners are the culture in a professional service firm. What the partners do and how they do it sets the tone for what gets done and how. By setting a personal example that embodies the firm's commitment to client value and delivery excellence, a firm's leaders ensure the continued support of their professionals to the firm and what it stands for. The activities that will deliver a positive personal example are:

- Displaying an unswerving commitment to market leadership

- Demonstrating passion and belief

- Treating everyone with dignity and respect

- Demonstrating the highest integrity

- Giving credit to others

- Taking responsibility for failure

Without the personal example of all the partners, the practice would not be where it is today. Not every partner got it right all of the time, but by trying and ultimately succeeding in operating in the right way, the partners and the associates have developed a passion about and belief in their ability not just to sustain their performance but to build on it. The honesty of feedback and the way it is delivered is part of the core set of behaviors that underpin the way the practice operates and what it believes in. Credit does not just belong to the partners but to everyone. Similarly, partners took responsibility when things didn't go according to plan. The associates expressed concern over what they perceived as a lack of pastoral care in the initial implementation of the new layering structure, and the partners acknowledged that it was their fault that they had failed to discern how the associates were feeling. As a result, the system was altered to address the associates' concerns.

Herbert Smith's real estate practice is clearly differentiated from its competitors, and its focus on direction, commitment, execution, and personal example facilitated this differentiation. By aligning its business and talent strategies and its organization, the practice has been able to build its reputation to the point where its performance has garnered industrywide recognition. Many PSFs try to differentiate themselves, but they end up with an amorphous reputation or an unclear point of difference. This is because alignment is lacking. They may do a great job of setting direction, for instance, but they fail to secure commitment. Because these two elements aren't aligned, some firm members go about their jobs without the enthusiasm and creativity that emerges when alignment is there. They execute unevenly, and though firm leaders have created a brilliant strategy designed to differentiate the firm, the output fails to illuminate this point of difference.

Alignment, therefore, should be on the mind of every firm leader. That goal, however, is only part of the challenge. Aligning professionals with a high need for achievement raises the bar, and, as we'll see in the next chapter, motivating these individuals requires insight into what makes them tick.

7

The High-Need-for-Achievement Personality

Motivating, Retaining, and
Developing Your Talent

A central tenet of this book is that the unique characteristics of PSFs—their tasks, organizational forms, and especially their people—require a holistic and integrative approach to leadership. We have argued that an integrated leadership model is essential for attracting, developing, and retaining top professionals in an era of increasing competition, change, and growth.

But who are these professionals? What drives them? Why are they always asking for more feedback, better coaching, and greater challenges? Why is it so difficult to get some professionals (particularly partners) to give younger professionals the feedback and mentoring they ask for? Finally, why do good professionals at all stages of their career leave the firm when by all appearances they are doing well? These are critical questions, especially for leaders in PSFs, where it is not a cliché to say that your people are your most important asset.

We intend to provide a deeper insight into the kinds of people who are attracted to PSFs, as well as their needs and motivational drivers. With this basis of understanding in place, we will then focus on the implications for the motivation, development, and retention of professionals—and what it means for those who lead them.

The Profile of the High-Need-for-Achievement Personality

As in other occupational groups, people who are attracted to the professions come with a wide range of dispositions, tastes, needs, and personality types. This diversity is reflected in the variety of people who can be found in PSFs. Nonetheless, there are a number of characteristics that distinguish people who are attracted to professions such as the law, medicine, public accounting, investment banking, advertising, and most types of consulting. Some of these characteristics include a high need for autonomy; a loathing of anything that feels bureaucratic; a strong desire for collegiality and inclusion, professional credibility; and a greater than average need for a sense of the big picture (i.e., how does our practice fit in with the firm's strategy, and where is our competition headed?).

The most prominent characteristic of people who are attracted to these professions is that they are significantly overrepresented by the "high need for achievement" personality.[1] High-achieving personalities overselect these professions in that they choose them with greater frequency than other occupations. They are also over-selected by PSFs, in that they comprise the vast majority of professionals whom these firms hire. In this respect, PSFs have great radar and instincts for spotting and selecting the personality with a high need for achievement.

This overrepresentation of this personality in PSFs has been borne out by our testing of professionals in public accounting, investment banking, corporate law, and consulting. We have consistently found that from 67 to 85 percent of these professionals score high in the need for achievement. These results occur whether we are working with midlevel associates, newly made partners, or senior partners with major practice leadership responsibilities. The pattern is also invariant by size of firm: it shows up in small elite firms as well as in global mega firms. The same pattern also appears in the testing we have done of participants in Harvard's Leadership in Professional Service Firms Program, which includes leaders from the entire gamut of professional services, from architecture to money management to advertising.

The need for achievement is one of three motivational drives identified by David McClelland and his colleagues.[2] The other two are the need for affiliation and the need for power. Technically known as the social motives, the three need drives are excellent indicators of the motivation to perform at work.[3] We focus on the need for achievement because it is the only one of the three that is characteristic of people who self-select into the professions. Professionals vary significantly in their needs for affiliation and power, so there is not as consistent a pattern in PSF professionals as there is with the need for achievement. Figure 7-1 provides a brief overview of each of the drives and of the activities, needs, and outcomes that each type finds inherently motivating to perform. Having a grasp of all three motivational need drives can be very useful in understanding how *in-*

FIGURE 7-1

Profile of motivation needs

Need for achievement *Task driven*	Need for affiliation *Relations driven*	Need for power *Influence driven*
• Having challenging tasks	• Interacting with others	• Influencing others
• Competing; striving to be number one	• Socializing as part of work	• Leading; providing direction
• Achieving task closure	• Being part of a team or group	• Building a team
• Setting goals and then meeting them	• Developing friendships and long-term relationships	• Shaping the organization
• Getting clear, timely, and actionable feedback	• Minimizing social disruptions or disagreements	• Developing others
• Being able to calibrate own performance		
• Having autonomy		
• Having control over task parameters		
• Taking calculated risks		

dividual colleagues are motivated and what their preferences are likely to be. Here, however, we will cover only those activities that characterize the high-need-for-achievement personality.

Motivational Drivers

People with a high need for achievement are motivated by many drivers, but at their core they are motivated to perform as well as possible. This is why they are known as the task-driven personality, as indicated in the figure. They are also motivated by several specific needs and activities.

Task Challenge

The most fundamental motivator is challenging work. For achievement-oriented personalities who self-select into the professions, the task challenge lies in solving complex problems and figuring out solutions to puzzling questions. For them, solving challenging questions—real puzzles for real clients—is motivating. This is their lifeblood. This kind of task challenge is very different from that which motivates the high-need-for-achievement personalities who self-select into entrepreneurial careers. (Entrepreneurship and the professions are the two occupational groups that are most over-selected by such personalities.) For entrepreneurs, the task challenge lies in the act of creation: making something that didn't exist before or creating something out of nothing—such as starting a business from the ground up, or buying a company, turning it around, and then selling it.[4]

These differences in what comprises the task challenge have significant implications for PSFs. High-achieving entrepreneurs, for example, will do anything it takes to get a new enterprise off the ground, including doing boring, repetitive, even tedious work, if it is in the service of creating a business. In contrast, high-achieving professionals become *un*motivated when the work is tedious, unless there is a very compelling reason to do it. If asked to do repetitive work on a sustained basis, they will eventually lose commitment and quit if they have the option. In PSFs the importance of task challenge is further complicated by the reality that practice-based PSFs function as stratified apprenticeships in which junior professionals expand their skills by learning and mastering new challenges on the job. However, what is a daunting challenge for a junior professional the first time soon becomes a source of mastery and pride by the fourth time; but by the twentieth time, it simply becomes tedious.

Being Number One

The high-need-for-achievement personality is motivated by the opportunity to compete. Such people try to be the best at whatever they're striving to do, whether it's being one of the best intellectual property litigators in health care or the best on the West Coast, or being one of the best third-year associates in the firm, and so on. They are also motivated by being part of an effort that is striving to become the best or one of the best in the business, such as belonging to a group that is doing the most exciting deals in the industry, litigating the most complex or high-stakes matters, or being the dominant or best consulting practice in a particular industry or niche.

Task Closure

Being achievement-oriented personalities, most professionals are motivated to get the task (deal, project, or matter) done as quickly and as effectively as possible. If the task involves getting from A to B, they are extremely impatient with anything or anyone that gets in the way or impedes the process. Any activity that doesn't directly contribute to the task's trajectory of getting from A to B tends to be seen as distracting or irrelevant. For partners and other senior professionals, this often includes taking the time to coach or mentor a junior professional, a few minutes to give quick, corrective feedback, or even ten seconds to acknowledge a junior's presence. Other partners become frustrated with organizational processes like performance evaluations and training. In this respect, the inherent impatience of a high-achieving personality with anything that does not directly contribute to a task's completion can have a number of negative as well as positive consequences, as we will elaborate on later.

Setting and Meeting Goals

Because such professionals *are* so task-driven and achievement-oriented, the very process of setting goals and then meeting them is inherently motivating. Even when professionals do not derive deep satisfaction by simply achieving a goal, they often will experience a sense of relief when the project is completed.

Clear, Timely, Actionable Feedback

High-need-to-achieve individuals have a much greater need for feedback than does the population as a whole. This is because they want to perform as well as possible, which in turn means getting feedback on what they are not doing well and what they can do to improve. Equally important—and motivating—is getting feedback on their overall performance.

Although high-achieving professionals, like everyone, prefer getting positive feedback, they need constructive negative feedback to perform better. Otherwise, they may spin their wheels in place and eventually become unmotivated. Our experience has been that though achievement-driven individuals hope for positive feedback, they deeply resent it when they don't get negative feedback that could have improved their performance. In many instances, this is reason enough for quitting a firm.

The point is that for such professionals, especially those at the junior level who are still learning how to do the work, not only is quality feedback a major source of motivation, it is also essential to their continued improvement. In this respect, leaders in PSFs who give their professionals ongoing constructive feedback are contributing both to the quality of execution and to the personal commitment of their people. This is a critical aspect of being an integrated leader, for it is *sine qua non* for junior and midlevel professionals to stay motivated and on track.

Self-Calibration

A related need of high-achieving professionals is self-calibration. Self-calibration means being able to determine how well they are doing in terms of their work and in comparison to others at their career stage. This is another aspect of their achievement drive, which means being as effective as possible in their work. Their ability to calibrate themselves accurately is closely related to the quality of feedback they receive (or don't receive). Many very high achievers will leave for other—sometimes lesser—opportunities if they feel they are unable to calibrate where they stand at their stage of career.

Autonomy

For high-need-for-achievement personalities, having the autonomy needed to do their work free of constraint is in and of itself a motivating force. Working on a challenging problem and having the running room to approach it creatively are a powerful combination for high-achieving professionals. Conversely, they become frustrated or unmotivated when limitations are imposed that interfere with their ability to deal directly with problems, or when these barriers reduce their degree of freedom. This is especially the case when they perceive such constraints as being needlessly bureaucratic.

Control over Task Parameters

The other side of having the autonomy needed to get the project done well is that most professionals also have a great need to control the task's parameters, such as the resources necessary to get the work done and the actual framework within which the project is defined. Like autonomy, having influence over these parameters is motivating and the lack of it is unmotivating or even frustrating. High achievers' need to control the task and its parameters tends to make them poor delegators. For most of these personalities, delegating is a learned skill rather than a spontaneous act. For many, delegation does not come easily.

Taking Calculated Risks

Finally, although achievement-oriented professionals typically do not experience themselves as risk takers, they are motivated by the opportunity to take calculated risks. The key word here is *calculated*, which is why they sometimes appear to be risk averse. This source of motivation is related to their need for task challenge, but they are motivated only by challenges that are realistic and achievable.

These drivers are the activities, actions, and outcomes that the high-need-for-achievement personality finds motivating. They are inherently motivating because the need for achievement is a personality disposition that is relatively stable. As such, the drive to achieve is an *internal source of motivation* as compared to an *extrinsic source*, such as compensation, status, or recognition, in which external rewards are used to induce performance. In this respect, high achievers are already induced to perform. Extrinsic rewards will amplify, diminish, or refocus their motivation to perform, depending on how aligned these rewards are with the motivational drivers just described. Extrinsic rewards seldom have a neutral effect on a high achiever's level of motivation, but they are not necessary to induce the motivation to perform. We should be explicit however: money does matter for professionals in PSFs. Unless there is a great deal of identification with and commitment to the firm, good professionals will leave for better monetary rewards, especially when combined with more challenging work. In addition, for highly competitive professionals, rewards such as compensation, bonuses, and so on are a clear way of keeping score and of calibrating how well they are doing.

What They Need to Stay Motivated

Based on the internal motivational drivers just described, a key question for leaders in PSFs is what do high-achieving professionals need to *stay* motivated? If we focus on professionals at the pre-partner levels, the list is fairly short.

Ongoing Tactical Feedback

Tactical feedback is aimed at pointing out what a professional is doing well and badly in real time, that is, during a project, engagement, or deal. This is an inherent aspect of the on-the-job training during a professional apprenticeship, and it is often given by more senior professionals, such as case managers, team leaders, or senior associates. For professionals at all levels, the most powerful feedback comes from partners. This kind of specific, actionable feedback not only addresses the high achiever's need for feedback but also results in real-time learning and improved performance. For an achievement-driven professional, then, it's a win-win situation. In addition, tactical feedback has the immediate effect of improving an individual's (and a team's) quality of execution. The attention that comes with this kind of online feedback also builds commitment. It is an integral aspect of integrative leadership.

The important point is that effective feedback must occur as close to the real-time performance as possible. One investment bank we worked with uses the expression, "Feedback on the run is better than none." It gives an associate immediate feedback on an error or dysfunctional pattern, even if the feedback feels rushed or is incomplete and leaves the associate slightly anxious. Waiting until later to give fuller feedback risks a situation in which the associate unknowingly continues to make the same mistakes. This trade-off is far better than waiting several weeks or days to deliver the feedback on a more planned and less hurried occasion. Often, neither the senior nor the junior professional will even remember the problem at that point; in the meantime, the younger professional has failed to correct the shortcoming, further impeding both performance and development.

In short, in terms of motivation, professional development, and performance, junior and midlevel professionals need feedback that is ongoing, on-the-job, and timely. Waiting to give feedback during an annually scheduled performance review often causes more frustration than motivation. The person receiving the review is often more focused on compensation and comparisons with peers than on any substantive developmental conversation.

Periodic Developmental Feedback

As mentioned earlier, constructive feedback on how a professional is generally performing, in terms of both strengths and areas that need improvement, is very motivating for high achievers. Effective developmental feedback also includes a discussion of an action plan that leads to further development and improved performance.

Almost all firms have periodic reviews of some kind. In many it is merely a pro forma process that focuses more on past performance than on developmental feedback aimed at improving future performance. In many cases it does not include actively planning the steps and resources needed to develop further. Firms that excel at giving quality developmental feedback, such as McKinsey and

Bain, also encourage their leaders to give informal developmental feedback between formal reviews.

Done well, developmental feedback is especially motivating for high-achieving professionals because it directly addresses the need to achieve as well as to improve or enhance performance. Constructive, actionable developmental feedback also enables such individuals to self-calibrate more accurately.

Coaching and Mentoring

It is common today to make a distinction between developmental feedback, which usually includes coaching by a professional's senior, and mentoring, which involves distinct career guidance. In general, the more senior high-need-to-achieve professionals become, the more they want the kind of mentoring that addresses the question, "What does it take to make it at this firm?" Such professionals both need and expect to get this kind of mentoring. Our experience has been that when they aren't mentored, they interpret this lack as a signal that they're already seen as lacking the potential to become a partner, or that the partners they work for simply don't care. Sometimes, this self-calibration is accurate, and the person will eventually leave or be advised to leave. But in many cases, it is not accurate, but the junior professional leaves—and the firm loses someone with the potential to make further contributions.

Developmental feedback and quality mentoring are both examples of integrative leadership at its best. Each of these actions achieves a number of important outcomes simultaneously. Developmental feedback and mentoring are not only highly motivating to the best professionals; they are also, if done well, both directly related to the professional development and retention of top professionals. Moreover, in mentoring and giving developmental feedback, integrative leaders provide direction at the personal level that helps professionals execute more effectively and secures their personal commitment to the firm.

Challenging Work

Challenging work is a major source of motivation for high-need-for-achievement personalities that self-select into professional work. The characteristics of such intrinsically motivating work include: (1) *challenging problems*; (2) the *opportunity to learn* from the work itself (e.g., developing new skills, gaining new insights); and (3) *acquiring experience that enhances them as professionals*. In addition, high achievers are also intrinsically motivated by (4) the process of *gaining mastery* over the problems posed by the work, as well as by (5) *a sense of closure*, that is, being able to complete an entire task, or at least knowing how their piece of a project fits into the total picture.

As a source of motivation, challenging work speaks for itself and needs little elaboration, except to reiterate a point made earlier. In a PSF, work that a professional initially experiences as so challenging that it's daunting the first time will soon become routine once mastered and boring the twentieth time around. In a PSF, boring and repetitive tasks are the enemies of challenging work.

As a result of this constant need for new challenges, excellent professionals sometimes become "plateaued" in their apprenticeship, because they are doing work that they have long since mastered. They're not learning anything new, and the work has become routine. We refer to this as a "flat spot" in their professional development, which can occur for many reasons. Most often, it is due to the nature of the client work in a given period, which involves activities that are no longer challenging. For example, M&A markets may be hot, creating a sustained demand for a lot of due diligence work, or a certain kind of customer relations management (CRM) product is in greater demand, resulting in an endless backlog of the same kind of work.

But there are various causes for being in a flat spot. The client-demand effect is quite different, for instance, from a situation in which a young professional is given an unending stream of a certain type of due diligence work; because she has learned to do it very well, her leader doesn't want to take the time to break in someone else to perform (and learn from) this type of work. In this case, the associate is in a flat spot not as a result of market demands but as a result of poor leadership. Sometimes, on the other hand, flat spots occur just before a professional is ready to move to the next rung of the apprenticeship, such as being promoted from being a manager in a Big Four accounting firm to becoming a senior manager. What-ever the cause, excellent professionals are most vulnerable to being picked off by a headhunter, a competitor, or a client—or simply leaving out of boredom—when they are in a flat spot.

Given that flat spots occur with greater frequency today than in years past, partners must be vigilant, acknowledge the situation, ex-plain why it is happening, and communicate the intention to give the professional more challenging work as soon as the deal or proj-ect flow changes. In the absence of such acknowledgment that he is mired in a flat spot, the professional will inevitably conclude that he is stuck because the firm does not believe he is capable of doing more challenging or demanding work or, even worse, that his cur-rent situation is a good predictor of what a career in the firm will be like—a lot of boring work. Either conclusion will result in top pro-fessionals leaving as soon as they can find a viable alternative. It's far better to acknowledge the flat spot and seek opportunities to give the person more challenging work.

Integrative leaders monitor where their people are in their ca-reers and do all that they can to ensure that good people don't stay in a flat spot for long. For high-achieving professionals, a lack of challenging work on a sustained basis predictably results in re-duced motivation and commitment, lack of development, and poor connection to the firm. For the firm, these are all negative out-comes.

Recognition

Although we have not discussed recognition per se, it is a powerful source of positive feedback and motivation for the achievement-driven professional. We do not mean recognition in the sense of giving prizes, awards, or banquets. Rather we are referring to situations in which leaders acknowledge or recognize a professional who has done an extraordinary job on a client project, has gone the extra mile, or has significantly enhanced an engagement team's perfor-mance. Unlike an award dinner, this kind of recognition takes place opportunistically, such as when a partner stops an associate or manager in the hallway to tell her how much he appreciates the great job she has done on her part of a project or transaction.

This kind of recognition occurs during personal interactions that may take only a minute or less, but nevertheless can be very powerful. For pre-partner professionals—regardless of level—this recognition, especially from a partner or other leader, is like a shot of jet fuel. A senior partner, recalling a similar experience when he was a third-year associate in a Wall Street law firm, described it as leaving him "walking three feet off the ground for the rest of the day" and "glowing for a month." These were his feelings thirty years ago, yet he recalled them as if they happened yesterday!

Recognition is one of the most underused sources of motivation in PSFs. Like any currency, however, if it is overused, it becomes de-based. If, for example, a partner shoots off an e-mail to members of his team after every meeting commenting on how great the session was, by the third such e-mail the gesture will have no value whatsoever. The effort will be viewed as insincere or stereotyped. But if brief recognition is used sincerely and when truly merited, it can be a powerful source of both motivation and commitment for high achievers. This kind of recognition requires no money and little time. What it does take is the thought to do it, which is why it matters to professionals so much.

Thus far our discussion of recognition has focused on nonpartner professionals only. It does not take much imagination, however, to see that the same kind of recognition given to a partner by a fellow partner or by a practice leader can be just as powerful and just as welcome.

In years past, PSF leaders have not been as concerned with coaching and mentoring responsibilities as with other aspects of their role. But as the need to motivate professionals increased along with the growing importance of development and retention, firm leaders began incorporating on-the-job feedback, work challenges, and other tactics into their integrated repertoire. They recognized that high-need-for-achievement professionals required more attention than they were receiving. They saw the need to secure commitment to the firm's direction as a way of increasing motivation and ensuring retention. And they understood that if they provided the young professionals with the feedback that helped them execute more effectively, both they and the firm would benefit.

The PSF Paradox

If what it takes to keep high-achieving professionals motivated and committed is so clear, why is it then that so few PSFs do it well? Perhaps the most common complaint heard from pre-partner professionals is that they get little or no on-the-job or developmental feedback. Junior associates often complain that team managers plan poorly, give little feedback, and seem constantly distracted and under pressure. They see senior associates who can't manage time and projects. They report that their interactions with partners are rare, and when they do occur, they are usually curt, distant, and focused only on the agenda of the partner.

The complaint most often heard from more senior, pre-partner professionals is that they get little or no mentoring. Partners seem too busy and preoccupied, or act as if they don't care. Another frequent lament is that neither their partners nor their firm are clear on what they need to master, prove, or otherwise demonstrate in order to have a crack at partnership or its equivalent. Many associates who depart firms note that the only honest career discussions they ever had occurred during their exit interviews.

One possible reason why these needs go unaddressed is that the personality with a high need to achieve can *never* get enough feedback. Partners also comment that the current generation of professionals demands more feedback and more flexibility than prior generations—that they are needier and less willing to work long hours or deal with ambiguities.

Although there are elements of truth to these and other explanations, we believe that the principal causes are far more fundamental. They have to do with the very nature of the high-need-for-achievement personality itself. Because professionals working their way up the stratified apprenticeship *are* high-achieving personalities, they have a high need for feedback and self-calibration. Paradoxically, partners and other senior professionals who also have high-need-for-achievement personalities are not disposed to give feedback to, coach, and mentor their juniors, precisely because they are impatient with everything that distracts them from the real work of getting from A to B—serving clients and enhancing the book of business. For many partners and other senior professionals, on-the-spot corrective feedback, coaching, and mentoring are not seen as central to the task trajectory of getting a project, deal, or matter done, so these aspects of leadership are ignored.

We call this self-feeding dynamic the "PSF paradox." The paradox is that because they too are high-achievement personalities, senior professionals are not disposed to give junior professionals what they need to stay motivated or develop—even though they too had the same needs early in their careers. This holds true for partners as well. Just because a partner is at midcareer doesn't mean there is less need for feedback. Professionals at all levels want to know that those responsible care about them and are interested in their development.

Lack of feedback is a critical issue in PSFs today, regardless of profession. We hear this complaint in all but the most well-managed firms. The misalignment between the professional needing feedback and not getting it is further amplified because most PSFs are apprenticeships in which constant learning, striving, and mastery are necessary to get ahead. Indeed, if one wanted to design an organization that would perpetually punish the high-need-for-achievement personality, the modern-day PSF would fit the bill. It guarantees that at any moment, at some level, a high-achieving professional will be in pain. The effects of the paradox are exacerbated by two other factors. The first is related to the achievement-driven personality itself; the second is related to the growth in professional services in the last decade.

Prisoners of the High Need for Achievement

One of the potential dangers of being a high-achieving personality is becoming a prisoner of the need for achievement. This is especially likely in PSFs where most leaders and senior professionals continue to produce. As a result, many senior professionals become prisoners of their own need to achieve. This may be the case even though they may be high in one or both of their other two principal needs: the *need for affiliation*, which is the motivation to interact, socialize, build relationships, and generally connect with others; and the *need for power*, which is the motivation to influence others, build a team, and lead and develop others. Both sources of motivation are highly conducive to providing the leadership and motivation in short supply in most PSFs. One would expect that partners high in either the need for affiliation or the need for power would be more effective in providing what junior professionals require.

The problem is that during the trajectory of getting the task done (the deal, matter, project, etc.), the need for *achievement* supersedes the other needs for affiliation and power. This is because the need for achievement is the task-driven need. The need to accomplish tasks and goals is simply more fundamental than the other two drives. As a result, high-achieving personalities are often captives of their need for achievement. This is why, for example, a senior partner who actually has a very high need for affiliation is unlikely to act very warm and friendly toward a junior working with him on a project.

There are two exceptions to this generalization. The first occurs when one or both of the other two needs are salient to accomplishing the task. For example, the need for affiliation is very important to the task of building a relationship with a client, while the need for power is useful in influencing a client. In both cases, the particular need will naturally be evoked because during the task, it serves to get the task done. Almost everyone who has had a career in professional services can remember being a junior associate working for a partner with whom all interactions were brief, curt, and to the point, only to discover during a social event or an after-hours drink that the partner was in fact gracious, warm, and funny. What the junior associate saw for the first time was the partner's need for affiliation, which wasn't evoked when they worked together because it wasn't salient for accomplishing the task.

The second exception to the generalization is when an individual has enough insight *not* to allow the need for achievement to block the other two needs while engaged with coworkers in doing the work. The need to achieve is a fairly stable personality disposition, so it is not a case of "use it or lose it." Senior professionals can choose consciously *not* to be prisoners of their need for achievement, but it is not easy.

Many senior partners are also high in their need for power, which is very much about influencing, leading, and building. They are naturally motivated to do the things that PSFs need and that strong leaders provide; unfortunately, their high need for achievement often blocks them from doing so. They forget to connect with associates when their schedules get out of control. They become overcritical when they feel they have too much to accomplish. They are so engrossed in the task that they don't take the two minutes needed to give on-the-spot corrective feedback, or even take five seconds to acknowledge the presence of a junior associate. When they free themselves from being captives of their need to achieve, they open themselves up to becoming much better leaders of their people and their organizations.

An integrated leader must stop being a captive of his or her need for achievement. Doing so is what enables senior professionals to see the leadership role holistically. That is, they can see their job not only in terms of focusing on execution, but also in terms of providing direction, building commitment, and exemplifying a great professional.

The Difficulty of Motivation and Development Today

Both the PSF paradox and the dominance of the need for achievement over other needs have existed in professional service firms for many years. Motivating and developing professionals, however, have become significantly more difficult tasks during the last decade. This is because the professional services industry has grown enormously during this period, while also becoming more competitive and, in most professional services, more profitable—at least as measured by profitability per partner, margins per partner-level equivalent, and margins per professional.

This drive for growth and greater per-partner profitability has resulted in greater scale and complexity, as well as greater leverage in terms of professionals per partner. In the past, for example, the leverage of many law firms was in the range of 1:2 to 1:3 (ratio of partners to associates); today it is in the 1:3 to 1:4 range in many practice segments, and even greater in others. Similarly, in IT consulting, leverage has grown from the 1:10 to 1:12 range to the 1:15 to 1:40 range.

The consequences of the increased size and leverage of today's PSF are that much of the feedback, coaching, and mentoring that took place naturally and spontaneously as part of client work a decade ago no longer occurs that way today. This is because the lower leverages and smaller practice groups that existed then enabled junior professionals to have much more contact with team leaders, partners, and other senior professionals than is possible today—a direct consequence of the increase in the numbers of professionals per partner.

In most PSFs, for example, it would have been unthinkable ten years ago for a talented third-year associate not to have caught the eye of at least a couple of partners. Today, it's entirely possible that this talented professional is flying under the radar. The differences in contexts—the greater size, complexity, competition, and leverage today—are among the reasons many partners are perplexed by the great hue and cry for more feedback and mentoring. Partners are focused more on adapting and adjusting to bigger firms themselves and often think less about reaching down to younger professionals.

The reality is that their junior associates are not getting as much feedback or mentoring as they themselves once did in the normal course of doing client work.

The combined effects of greater leverage, growth in size, and increased scale have had a "tipping" effect: they have rendered the naturally functioning, stratified apprenticeship and the old leadership models no longer viable. In the past, there were enough broadly effective senior professionals in most practices to keep their high-need-for-achievement professionals motivated, engaged, and developing. Despite the paradoxical consequences of the concentration of achievement-driven personalities in PSFs and the negative effects of the predominance of the achievement need over other needs, most professionals got enough attention because seniors routinely worked with juniors. Since this situation has changed, however, many professionals do not receive coaching, mentoring, and motivation, creating huge development and retention challenges. The psychological and emotional connection simply does not exist between many partners and associates. As a result, some junior professionals are less committed to their firms today.

Integrative Leadership and Motivation

The convergence of these factors creates the need for a more explicit and holistic model of leadership in today's professional service firms and a new holistic, integrated approach. This convergence may cause PSF leaders to wonder how they can both differentiate their firms and hold on to their talent more effectively. By introducing the integrated leadership model, we underscore the need for a different kind of leadership paradigm that confronts the current PSF problems head on. High-need-for-achievement personalities must believe that others worry about their careers. They must know that leaders empathize with them and understand that they are pulled in many directions.

As we have noted, leaders will have difficulty meeting these challenges if they are focused only on execution. As much as they must help their professionals execute effectively, they cannot neglect setting direction and securing commitment. If they neglect these responsibilities, execution will be affected negatively. Integrated leaders seize every opportunity to secure buy-in to firm strategy, providing the motivation to help professionals achieve their potential along with firm objectives.

Similarly, setting a strong personal example has a multifaceted effect on associates and other professionals. Firm leaders who lead holistically—who set direction, secure commitment, and execute—model an alternative for young professionals. They demonstrate that despite their desire to achieve great things, they also make time to inspire, motivate, and develop associates. This personal example helps increase the likelihood that young professionals moving up will also be integrated leaders.

Now let's turn to another group of professionals who also have a high need to achieve. As essential as B players are to professional service firms, they are often overlooked and underappreciated—and sometimes are not given the opportunity for achievement at all. This is a large and critical group of professionals who are loyal, hard working, and committed to the profession. However, because they are not the stars of the firm, they often fly under the radar screen.

8

The Essential B Player

The Heart and Soul of an Organization

In professional service firms today, A players demand attention, C players look for anchors of security, and solid, B-class professionals are often overlooked and underappreciated.[1] If the A players comprise the top 10 percent of a firm's professionals and its C players comprise the bottom 15 percent, then, by definition, a firm's B players comprise 70 to 75 percent of its professionals. All firms, including those in the top tier, have a large majority of B players who are often the heart and soul of the organization. Consider how much time, attention, and effort you are devoting to the great majority of your professionals—the solid middle. If your B players are mediocre, your firm will be mediocre. If they are high performers, your firm will be high performing. A players, comprising only

15 percent of any firm's population, will never make up for the 70 percent in the middle, regardless of how good they are. And there will always be that 70 percent in the middle.

Alarmingly, PSFs that do not recognize these B players fail to maximize their considerable value. Because they are largely self-sufficient and secure about who they are and tend to be aware of their roles and responsibilities, B players typically need less care and feeding than A or C players. However, this lack of recognition of professionals who are not in the top or bottom 10 percent can seriously weaken a service firm. Part of the problem, of course, is that leaders unfairly view B players as not ambitious and unable to perform at the top level; they perceive them as lacking the drive to be stars. Everything from the popular press to admonitions from our society's collective unconscious reinforces this stereotype. In reality, managing partners may not understand the motivation of solid contributors because B players are in fact different from the managing partners and, therefore, less understood.

The challenge to PSFs is to overcome this stereotypical thinking, recognize the significant contributions of B players, and capitalize on these contributions. If the contributions of the solid citizens in a firm are not recognized over time, eventually the B player will see himself as a C player. At that point, the firm will have a management problem.

Integrated leaders recognize and respond to the value of B players. They make a consistent effort to secure the B players' commitment to the firm's direction and give them the necessary resources. Above all, they integrate B players into the mix. Rather than taking them for granted, they take a personal, active interest in them and communicate their importance to the firm's success. Leaders understand that with just a modicum of recognition, these professionals become even more committed to the enterprise.

A Silent but Significant Majority

During a conversation with his personal coach, Jason, a high-level division head in a large financial services firm, recognized that he was neglecting his B players. After reviewing Jason's daily work journal, the coach advised Jason that virtually all his time was occupied by high-flying star players and, to a much lesser extent, low performers. Jason seemed to fill his day worrying about retaining and satisfying the stars, while at night he worried about his low performers, because he didn't know what to do with them. Jason was effectively ignoring 70 percent of his division all the time. These B-level professionals were competent, loyal, high-need-for-achievement personalities who supported the firm's vision, spoke out about its faults and failings, and were not psychologically draining him or others. Jason realized that they took much less attention from their leaders and demanded fewer resources. They went about their work in a professional manner. They remained with the organization longer, had more institutional knowledge, and took more time reaching out to other professionals. It began to dawn on Jason just how invaluable these B-level professionals were and how much he had ignored them.

PSFs unconsciously organize their people into three groups. Through benign neglect, they tend to forget those in the middle, the solid performers who are the institutional anchors of the firm. It is on the backs of their B players that professional service firms achieve higher utilization rates. Only when firms recognize the value of their B players can they begin to enhance their roles or at least reframe the importance of these solid performers.

Contrary to conventional wisdom, B players cannot be ignored indefinitely. Though they might not cause problems or act like prima donnas, they require at least a modicum of attention. If firms ignore the 70 percent who comprise the solid middle, they not only diminish their effectiveness short-term, they also cannot expect them to remain loyal forever. When firms lack systems or processes for tracking the B players' development, or fail to enlighten the senior professionals who ignore them, they lose touch with their silent majority.

Start Paying Attention to B Players . . . and Stop Them from Leaving

No one at Morgan Stanley would have identified Catharine Chung (not her real name) as a star. After eleven years in the investment banking division, Catharine was promoted to managing director in the financial institutions group, where she followed up on bankers' work and ensured that transaction structures and terms were optimized. She was viewed as an excellent technician, utterly loyal to the firm, a valuable mentor to junior professionals, detail-oriented, and focused on clients that were for the most part internal to the firm. Although Catharine was not seen as a star, she was viewed as invaluable to Morgan Stanley.

In time, Catharine needed a new challenge. She felt that she had been doing the same thing for too long and that she was no longer learning. When she articulated her career frustrations, her superiors emphasized that she was doing a good job and urged her to continue at it, because the firm needed her in that role. Although she loved the firm and the people, Catharine could not envision spending another ten years in the same position. She began seriously to consider career options outside the firm.

When Catharine's counterpart in Morgan Stanley's London office requested a transfer to New York, management asked if she would be interested in the London position. She accepted the offer. Energized by the relocation and the new professionals with whom she was engaged, Catharine quickly assumed additional managerial responsibilities and began mentoring more junior professionals. After two years in London, she was moved into a leadership position that had opened suddenly in the Paris office. Catharine headed the office for three years—overseeing two hundred professionals who covered myriad investment banking functions—before returning to New York. Though she was still not a superstar, she had proved herself to be an excellent office head and a highly competent and steady hand. Everyone in the firm trusted Catharine and valued her contributions as a producer and a manager.

Morgan Stanley was fortunate. Fate intervened when an opening occurred in the London office, and it was exactly the right development and growth opportunity for Catharine. If this opening had not occurred, Catharine in all likelihood would have left the firm. Instead, after stabilizing and energizing the Paris office, Catharine remained with the firm and continues to be highly effective and respected.

Many PSFs are blind to the value they can extract from B players such as Catharine. People like Catharine exist in every firm, and more often than not, they are taken for granted. Undervaluing these professionals eventually causes them to see themselves as C players. When this happens, the firm and the individual lose; the end result is often disenfranchisement, and the individual leaves the firm.

The Cycle of Disenchantment

B players need to be understood relative to their performance. Some undoubtedly have the potential to be A players, but because they are ignored, their talents are not leveraged. In addition, few firms reward managers for developing subordinate professionals' talents. When a solid performer is ignored, a vicious cycle ensues. Managers focus on A players—especially the squeaky wheels who demand additional responsibilities and attention—or the C players who need coaching or additional help because their performance is clearly below standard. Meanwhile, they ignore the B players who don't ask for attention and seem to function competently without any mentoring, coaching, or other forms of development. The result? B players eventually feel neglected or come to see themselves as low performers.

With this vicious cycle in play, many leaders assume that the answer to their firms' people problems involves recruiting better talent from outside the firm—neglecting a large group of capable performers who are already hired and want development. The managers give up too quickly on the people they already have. Afforded few internal job alternatives because they are seldom on the radar screen in management's career planning meetings, solid performers become discouraged because they feel both overlooked and underappreciated. Perception dictates their reality: being perceived as beneath notice, they begin to act less secure, less proactive, and more like victims of the organization.

Ideally, senior professionals should intervene before their B players become discouraged or frustrated. But they usually avoid such uncomfortable conversations, because they have not been trained to give tough but actionable feedback, or because they are consumed by their A players. Other managers are too quick to slap labels on people, assuming that B performers who become discouraged will never be able to improve. They rarely reflect on whether a given professional can be developed or has the potential to grow. Instead, they rationalize their managerial approach, telling themselves that Max or Maya will never be anything more than a middle-of-the-road performer, and then prematurely search for people solutions outside the firm.

Leaders who adopt this "outsider" mind-set begin to think that all answers to the firm's talent problems involve lateral hires. Ignored, the younger professionals perceive that they have been forsaken by leaders who suffer from a variation of the "grass is always greener" syndrome. They are demoralized to see the firm's leaders placing more faith in unknown outsiders than insiders—whom the leaders should know but haven't taken the time to do so.

Finally, the cultural imperatives implicit in fast-paced, high-powered professional service firms play against solid performers finding long-term satisfaction. Because they haven't pushed for another job and have remained in a given position for a long time, they are often mistakenly perceived to lack drive or the ability to master new tasks. Firms inadvertently penalize these loyal B players by giving them passable evaluations or by overlooking their potential and contributions; thus their value frequently goes untapped. Worse, A players who are used to the limelight become critical of them for not being as committed or achievement driven as they are.

Why It Pays to Have B Players

Many leaders at professional service firms don't understand what makes B players tick. To foster your own understanding, consider the following traits. B players tend to:

- define success in broader terms than individual success (i.e., they view success as meeting the goals of the practice and firm, not just as achieving personal objectives);

- live relatively reasonable lives that have some semblance of balance over time;

- display stronger loyalty to their firms than the high flyers;

- take pride in and are apostles for the firm's brand (to the point of putting the firm's needs ahead of their own career considerations);

- believe in the organizational community;

- exhibit extraordinary patience with career development processes and the managers who frequently overlook them.

This list suggests several advantages for firms that pay attention to their solid performers. When the organization is working like a well-oiled machine, B players feel successful; they don't need constant praise or perks to derive satisfaction from their work. They are also satisfied when their colleagues are coordinating and cooperating. They often have a healthier sense of self and are more psychologically grounded than some A or C players, and they possess the internal strengths to see and respond to the needs of others. They take the time to mentor, coach, and counsel instead of focusing only on their own personal achievements. Interestingly, some leaders we have known in PSFs tend to respond negatively to these positive behaviors, seeing them as being unnecessarily altruistic.

B players pursue organizational goals because they want to create stability for the firm and themselves in the long term. Their presence serves to ground the charismatic A players, who can sometimes destabilize the organization, and shore up the C players who might otherwise flounder. Although B players may not generate the most revenue or snare the most lucrative clients, they also will not endanger the company or embarrass the institution. Rather, their solid performance is what keeps the organization grounded and balanced.

Because they tend to be less politically savvy than A players and less astute at pushing their own agendas and advancing their own careers, B players are more likely to be perceived as naive. Some A players may not consider them to be real players or members of the club. Yet, it is the ability of these individuals to maintain perspective that keeps them focused on doing their work. B players often balance the neediness of the star players against the desperation of the underperformers.

Paying *Productive* Attention
to Solid Performers

The war for talent can cause some managers to neglect B players, when in fact it should prompt them to pay more attention to this neglected majority. When leaders focus most or all of their attention on recruiting stars from elsewhere and spend relatively little time searching for potential stars within their own ranks, they fight a losing battle.

Unfortunately, except in the very best managed firms, B players aren't provided with good opportunities or developed in any meaningful way. Instead, they are thrown into jobs at all levels and told to adapt. Socialization processes, if they exist, are often so ill-conceived that they hardly create aspirational environments for entry-level and lateral hires. To management, B players appear to be struggling or to lack A player potential. In reality, they have hit the B player ceiling because of the environment in which they perform. Or they may lack the political savvy to draw the attention of the key power brokers. The following approaches can help PSFs maximize B player contributions.

Cultivate New A Players

One traditional firm we have worked with has launched a career planning program for all people, not just stars. The firm's career development committee (CDC) assesses the development needs and progress of its people, who are matched with openings and new responsibilities throughout the more than twenty locations in which it operates. More importantly, it looks for B players who might become A players through stretch assignments.

Previously, the local leaders and the firm's top leaders had groomed high performers. The leaders, however, were disinclined to put their reputations on the line for individuals who might take

179

more time to adjust to a higher level of responsibility. As a result, the senior-level mentors tended to advocate only for clearly rising stars. They also felt pressure to create exciting career paths for the future leaders to prevent them from leaving the organization. Few had the time to seek creative openings for B players.

The CDC's more organized process of career development is now helping many solid performers receive the grooming and attention they need to succeed. Each B player now is assigned to an A player, who sees the task as contributing to the growth and development of the strong but not spectacular B players.

Track Interactions

The head of the investment banking division of a leading investment bank learned that some of his twenty-plus direct reports were feeling alienated and resentful that others got most of his attention. Discovering that he had no idea who was receiving the most attention, the division head began to track his interactions with the bankers. After monitoring his interactions for a short time, he saw a pattern emerge. Certain high-performing managing directors visited the division head frequently to express concerns or demand more resources. A couple of managing directors who were considering leaving the firm called weekly for career coaching. At least half of his direct reports, though, never initiated contact with him. They simply met with clients, managed projects, and supervised professionals. At first, they began to feel ignored and taken for granted. Later, they expressed their frustration. The division head subsequently used his practice of tracking interactions to ensure that his schedule included regular meetings and dinners with all his direct reports.

The division head realized that stars demand more attention than can reasonably be given. He now understood that this demand is a star reflex—a response to their genetic makeup, their substantial contributions to the bottom line, and their need to feel unique and superior to their peers. Managers who pander to stars' demands at the expense of their largely silent, undemanding, but solid performers jeopardize organizational stability and risk losing good people. Tracking interactions is a hedge against pandering. By recording who receives the most time, leaders can avoid neglecting the less demanding but no less valuable professionals.

Recognize the Silent Majority

The substantial contributions of B players can be acknowledged in various ways. For example, each week, leaders might send a solid performer who is doing a particularly good job a thank-you note via e-mail or call or even visit personally. Leaders can send the partner or a particularly solid professional some tickets to a concert or sporting event; they might also take solid performers to dinner or invite them to meet and discuss their work with the chairman. Whatever is done, a system should be devised for tracking who has been recognized and who has not. Assistants of leaders can monitor the diaries, journals, and calendars of their bosses and create a matrix highlighting the person with whom the leader has had the interaction and the frequency. It is critical that leaders be more aware of their behaviors so that good professionals do not pay the price for their lack of awareness.

Be Slow to Categorize

Too many new entrants to a firm are categorized as "mistake" hires or low performers, without being given time to develop. Trying to establish which professionals are likely to become high performers within a few months stacks the deck against those who develop slowly. The latter are tendered poorer assignments and inferior mentors, while fast starters receive mentoring from the firm's stars, who secure for them the best assignments, projects, and opportunities. The wind blows in the face of the low performer and at the back of the fast starter.

Slow evaluations, therefore, increase the odds for B-performer success. With fast evaluations, slow but steady professionals are categorized as lacking in some way, and even those labeled as fast starters often become burdened with unrealistic expectations. During the thirty years we have been observing and working in professional service firms, we have witnessed many young professionals and lateral hires categorized as low performers far too early in their career development. A young associate categorized as a low performer based on a brief interaction with a senior professional will soon have that reputation throughout the organization. Whether the evaluation is accurate is irrelevant.

Professionals make instant judgments for many reasons. They value quick assessments in time-sensitive situations and are confident of their ability to size up any situation or individual. Assessments rarely take into account the context. New associates learn at different speeds and in different ways. They respond to managers and mentors—and to the socialization process—differently. In many PSFs, however, leaders judge people based on their own experiences. How they responded to a given situation early in their careers is how they expect everyone to respond. They fail to recognize that in increasingly diverse cultures, professionals exhibit a wide variety of approaches to problems and opportunities; what works for one might not work for another. Sadly, because many leaders are fast-rising stars, they can be overly judgmental of professionals who have different working styles or different needs.

Lateral hires who are solid but not spectacular performers also suffer from the rush to judgment. A managing director left a prestigious firm for another that lacked any system or processes for connecting new hires to its social and political webs. The partner was neither visited by other partners nor assigned an assistant. Because he was not perceived as brilliant or star material, none of the leaders attempted to help him with his transition. He was not invited to the sector's annual party. He responded to this neglect by becoming more introverted; he was quickly perceived as aloof and arrogant. Within two months, he returned to his old firm where he was once again highly productive.

Leaders need to create a network of people who give them perspective and can tell them when they are being too quick to judge. The review processes should include HR experts who ensure that the young professionals are not judged too harshly on limited information.

Assumptions about the Contributions of Solid Performers

PSFs must be alert for dysfunctional evaluation patterns and recognize how they harm both individuals and firms. Firm and practice leaders have to recognize that whatever else drives them, professionals expect their work to hold meaning. They thrive in the presence of leaders who acknowledge their existence and manage them professionally. This is as true for solid performers as it is for stars.

Leaders must also learn to see and value the strong contributions of solid performers who have competencies crucial to the organization's viability. B players do not ask much, so management receives a significant return by investing a little time and recognizing contributions. Absent recognition, unqualified loyalty can turn into frustration that, over time, can precipitate a downward spiral to C-player performance, or the departure of a good professional for no apparent reason.

Enlightened managers plan time for and track their interactions with these professionals, recognizing that they require regular communication if they are to feel valued. Loyal, self-regulating B players can provide the necessary grounding for their organizations as competition intensifies, technology advances, and speed becomes increasingly critical to overall success. Because B players remain longer and build up institutional knowledge, they are invaluable when firms merge, downsize, or open new offices.

B players have a long-term perspective because they experience cycles and understand the ebbs and flows of organizational life. They can tell war stories, give examples of the organization's response, and most important, spend time and energy with other professionals. Too often, star performers are too busy to connect with others or to coach or give feedback to a junior professional working on their project. B players connect and create a psychological safety net that provides grounding for professionals so they can focus on their work.

Firms do not consciously devalue B players; rather, the following four erroneous assumptions cause devaluation:

1. *Everyone wants to be promoted to lead the firm.* The assumption that everyone wants to rise to a position of prominence is one that most firm leaders share because it is what motivates them. In contrast, many B players may be perfectly happy to remain in place if they are given other rewards and recognitions—challenging work, pats on the back, increased responsibility, additional perks. This doesn't mean that they don't want to become partners. They just don't want to be managing partners leading a major practice area, or the first one across the finish line. They typically want to do good work for the client and the firm, which they find satisfying by itself.[2]

2. *Everyone wants to be a manager.* Without creative career planning practices and incentive or reward systems, many leaders assume that professionals are rewarded by giving

them management responsibilities (and indirectly requiring that they forsake some of their technical competencies and the client work they value). B players often derive their greatest job satisfaction from their expertise; using their talents to deal with challenging situations is what motivates them—not the opportunity to lead a practice.

3. *Everybody wants the same thing from their work.* Because individuals choose organizations, leaders often assume that their own personal motivations are the same as everyone's; they assume that we are all the same. They may be driven by status, power, and money, but other high-need-for-achievement personalities may prefer working in relative autonomy or being allowed to use their creativity to solve client problems. That is, after all, why they chose to become professionals. While B players want to be fairly compensated, their goals often are not to make the most money in the firm. Their ambitions may be satisfied in other ways, and as a leader, it's important that you discern those ways.

4. *All professionals want to devote all their energy to the firm.* Implicit in this assumption is that professionals, by definition, reserve little energy for activities, people, and passions outside the workplace. In fact, some B players may be more well rounded than A players. They may have achieved a balance between their personal and professional lives that ultimately increases their value to firms. They are typically level-headed and maintain perspective, qualities that some work-obsessed A players may lack.

During volatile times, B players usually hunker down and remain in place, providing the firm with continuity and stability. In the same vein, B players are often great team players who are able to work well on diverse teams and to build and maintain relationships and alliances crucial in an interconnected world.

The tendency, however, is to focus on only those star performers who demand attention and bring in the most work. While celebrating their victories and acknowledging their extraordinary talents, at the same time, push A players to reach out to the invaluable solid performers who may do their work in unobtrusive ways.

B players hold the firm together in subtle yet profound ways. Ignore their efforts, their hard work, and their focus on the well-being of the firm at your peril. From our perspective, more and more PSFs are imploding because professionals at all levels do not feel included and connected to the community of the firm. Those firms that focus on the particular talents of B players in meaningful ways will sustain long-term success that benefits not only the institution but the professionals. The bulk of any firm's talent is its B players—the 70 percent who are neither stars nor failures but consistently solid performers. They *are* the firm, and the firm is only as good as they are.

In chapter 9, we emphasize how firms can become high performing through the process of connection. The challenge of connection permeates all firms in myriad ways. We tie this powerful process into the integrated leadership model.

9

The Challenge of
Connection

Connecting the Firm to the Future

One of the greatest challenges facing professional service firms today is the challenge of connection—connecting professionals to the firm. Many professionals today report being underutilized and bitter, working only for security in the form of a paycheck. The relationship between professionals and senior management can feel increasingly exploitative. Massive layoffs by many PSFs to cope with economic downturns during the bad times, combined with manifold ineptitude at socializing people into firms, have created a climate where commitment is low. Further, many professionals complain that achieving financial security will take nearly twice as long to achieve as in the past.

As Peter Drucker has observed, "All organizations now say routinely, 'People are our greatest asset.' Yet few practice what they preach, let alone truly believe it. Most still believe what nineteenth-century employers believed: people need us more than we need them. But, in fact, organizations have to market membership as much as they market products and sources—and perhaps more."[1] Drucker here provides a mere glimpse of the iceberg's tip. He goes on to reveal a bit more of the iceberg by suggesting that today's climate of disenchantment and distrust makes it more difficult than ever before to attract, retain, reorganize, reward, motivate, serve, and satisfy people.

The challenge of connecting professionals to the firm is only going to grow. The volatility that we're witnessing in the early twenty-first century is going to become more volatile. As work becomes virtual and global, disconnection threatens. It is incumbent upon leaders to recognize that professionals want to be included and connected to the soul of the firm.

Firms incur enormous financial costs when they are unaware of this critical dynamic. In this climate, the integrated leadership model is extremely useful. Integrated leaders who set direction, secure commitment, ensure execution, and set a strong personal example naturally connect professionals to their firms. If they exhibit these behaviors consistently, leaders can more than offset the disconnecting elements plaguing firms today. When professionals understand and commit to the firm's direction, they naturally feel more linked to the firm than when they're simply following orders.

What's at Stake

To understand the disenchantment of professionals who feel disconnected from their firms, consider their common beliefs:

- The perception that their talents are being underutilized, and they are not growing, developing, or keeping pace with their friends in other organizations.

- A sense that they lack a voice in their future at the firm.

- The conviction that their bosses are uncertain what to do with them—some new associates report that once they begin working, they rarely see the people they met during the hiring process.

- A feeling that no one in the organization cares about or is watching over their career. As one new associate remarked, "Is anyone other than me worried about my success?"

- The observation that being involved in recruiting is not valued by the firm's leadership; they only pay lip service to it.

Disconnection has emotional and psychological consequences, but it can also have economic costs. Firms that lose professionals incur significant costs in terms of economic opportunity. Not only do they waste the investment they made in training people, but they may also lose clients and junior professionals who sometimes follow departing professionals to their next firms. Morale suffers too as word gets out that exiting professionals were shunned and ignored with poor assignments and little resource support on the way out. Managers are often in denial about the economic cost of turnover, ignoring the fact that they are losing a quantifiable value—well-paid recruiters from the organizations among which they shuffle migrating professionals can attest to this value.

Knowledge is also lost when a solid performer exits a firm. While some specialized knowledge can be transferred to other people or into databases, a significant amount leaves with the professional and ends up in the hands of the individual's new employer—often a competitor.

Replacements can take months or years to get up to speed. When the number of professionals lost runs into the tens or hundreds, a firm's intellectual capital is staggeringly diminished. If this turnover occurs over a sustained period of time, a firm begins to lose any sense of differentiation or identity.

Executives under intense pressure to impress analysts and shareholders, however, do not always acknowledge these issues. Perhaps they would pay more attention to the problem of lost knowledge if they were aware of a few salient studies. For instance, the American Management Association found that "fewer than half of the firms that have downsized in the past five years have subsequently increased their profits and . . . only a third have reported higher productivity." Furthermore, the *Wall Street Journal* reported that "downsizing firms outperform the S&P 500 only slightly during the six months following news of a restructuring, then lag badly, netting a negative 24 percent by the end of three years."[2]

According to class data for Harvard Business School, only 36 percent of the students are still in their first jobs ten years later; 39 percent have held two jobs, and 21 percent three jobs.[3] These statistics would seem to corroborate Frederick Reichheld's observation that "some executive recruiters advise that a change of job every three to four years is an absolute necessity for the kind of résumé that will appeal to a modern corporation."[4] Perhaps. But enormous costs are associated with job hopping, and not just in terms of replacing lost employees. Reichheld estimates that the upfront cost of hiring a trainee is more than $50,000. "Counting fixed costs and capital costs," he continues, "the total outlay involved in bringing a new investment broker to the point of profitability exceeds $100,000. By the second year, the new brokers will earn about $25,000 as a contribution toward their own fixed costs. They won't earn any real profit for the firm until their third year."[5] What value is extracted from professionals who change jobs every three to four years if they only begin to earn profits for their employers in their third or fourth years? Add to this the cost of recruitment, which can reach almost astronomical levels.

Some job movement is part of the career journey, but firms do not have to accelerate this movement to the point that it becomes counterproductive to their bottom line. Despite solemn acknowledgments of the importance of human capital in annual reports and at CEO luncheons, firms' actual talent management practices do not always reflect this belief.

At one prestigious investment bank, a solid performer was hired as a new managing director to fill a critical gap in the investment banking division. While the firm was thrilled to have him join the ranks, the firm knew he wasn't a star performer. But his reputation for solid, consistent work over time made him the type of professional who would add great value to the firm. He understood client service and was well respected in his sector. The division head assumed that after he was hired, the mergers and acquisitions department would watch over him. Caught up in other tasks, the M&A leaders were surprised when after two months, the managing director left the firm and went back to his original firm. When asked why he left, he stated, "In two months, not one other managing director has come by to introduce himself, and I haven't been assigned an assistant yet. I made a big investment to join your firm, and I realized rather soon that self-promotion and making demands of senior managers is the only way to get ahead here. That is not how I do business. I don't have the time and energy to spend the next fifteen years of my life socializing myself into this system."

Like many PSF executives, the leaders had failed to institutionalize a process that would have made professionals feel part of the firm. This new managing director should have been offended, and he was. The experience made the division head rethink how much time was spent ministering to the needs of professionals who demanded the most or made the most noise. As we saw in chapter 8, leaders worry about the star performers during the day and the low-performers by night. This division head realized that he had forgotten the middle cadre of professionals who meant so much to the firm's long-term viability. Losing one had alerted the firm to the potential cost of losing many.

Recognizing and Responding to the Right Questions

Professionals at all levels question their standing relative to their colleagues. This is a reflection of normal insecurities; people want to know how they are perceived and valued. Unfortunately, many professionals never receive answers. Too often, their bosses are preoccupied with responding to tremendously challenging business concerns. Rapid firm growth coupled with increasingly volatile business environments pose new social and psychological challenges for leaders. In the current business model of greater market share, intense merger and acquisition activity, and rapid technological advances, how are scope and scale to be achieved? How are resources to be leveraged? How is a firm to stay true to its business and economic models?

As a result of today's market pressures, firm leaders are addressing business-related issues rather than facilitating stronger connections of professionals with the firm. Instead, leaders should address these questions:

- How can I attract, win, and keep the best professionals for the long term?

- How do I get the right people to leave at the right time and with the right attitude?

- How can I attract, win, and keep managers who can inspire their people as well as do the work?

- What does it take to get new professionals to commit for the long term?

For many years, leadership and management in PSFs have been subordinated to an emphasis on production, bringing in new clients, and making the numbers. Based on informal interviews with over one hundred upper-middle and senior partners in PSFs, these priorities often remain in place to the detriment of the connection between professional and firm. The managing director at an investment bank, for instance, lamented his responsibility for managing a group of associates and vice presidents, complaining that "management interferes with my real work." "How," he asked, "can I focus on clients and spend time internally at the same time? Management means bureaucracy . . . Too much management will stifle the entrepreneurial spirit."

The challenge of connection and inclusion relates to the scope and scale of the organization as well. "It's just not the same anymore since we've grown to over six hundred fifty lawyers," remarked one professional. "I don't feel like I can go to senior management anymore. They are just too busy. We used to feel like family here. Everyone was involved. We would stay until midnight working together on projects. Now we are beginning to feel like a corporation. Some of my close friends are leaving for better incentives and responsibility. How do we recapture that old spirit?"

Some junior professionals believe that the growing size of firms is inconsistent with maintaining elite status. They believe that greater regimentation and more rules follow scope and scale, and that size begets bureaucracy and bureaucracy frustrates their ability to do their work. Others see their colleagues moving to Silicon Valley or involved in hedge funds, private equity firms, or venture capital opportunities that accommodate greater involvement and input. "Why would I want to work most weekends and late into the night for the next three or four years," opined one, "while my friends are having more dynamic and lucrative careers?"

Ambitious junior professionals look for every sign, real or imagined, to chart their progress. They want to determine if they are on track, ahead of schedule, or in trouble. This job self-assessment can start as early as the first few weeks on the job, especially if they are struggling. These young associates are often savvy about the advancement process, recognizing that supervising professionals are looking for the brightest of the bright to leverage, and that they begin labeling new recruits in the first few days of work.

Technical competence is one of the key indices of a productive PSF career. Advancing through the organization on time with one's colleagues is the second key career variable. The third factor is how to keep individual professionals feeling included and connected.[6]

The Dimension of Inclusion

All professionals ask themselves: "Am I in the know?" "Am I being included?" "Am I in the club or out?" Career frustration almost invariably is related to feeling left out. Professionals at any level who believe that they no longer count lose confidence and begin to question their abilities. They often turn inward and obsess about their careers. A firm's culture determines where the boundary of inclusion is set. Who feels left out? Who isn't invited to meetings? Who lacks representation in key decision-making processes?

Of the three career-related dimensions, the boundary of inclusion often has the greatest impact on professionals. Those who feel outside the boundary turn inward, exacerbating the debilitating feeling of being left out. Professionals who sense their exclusion begin to with-

194

draw, looking for slights and convincing themselves that they are on the outside looking in. Colleagues are often aware of this withdrawal and may join other professionals in pointing fingers at professionals for isolating themselves or not getting work done. The professional's career trajectory plateaus, sputters, and veers off course.

To help professionals escape this counterproductive, vicious cycle of feelings and behaviors, leaders must intervene at the right time. If the cycle is permitted to continue and the only possible solution is outplacement, the firm loses a valuable resource.

Though each of the three factors impact the professional, the boundary of inclusion is becoming increasingly critical as the business world in general and professional services firms in particular experience greater volatility and ambiguity. In unpredictable, paradoxical times, professionals need a sense of connection more than ever.

Eldon Ernst was a senior partner at a large multinational financial services firm. In his late forties, he had been with the firm for twenty years. Eldon was very competent at executing the business but did not know how to create new business. Other professionals saw him as a solid performer, but not one of the power players. Fewer and fewer associates wanted to work with him because he was not regarded as someone who could get them promoted.

When a new department head was needed, a more junior partner who was seen as a true star was selected. She didn't know what to do with Eldon. She couldn't relate to him, not only because he was older but also because he was not a star like herself. She focused on creating more work by developing new clients, and the work poured in. The associates were drowning in work. A couple of associates quit, and another became sick. The department head worked harder than ever and began to resent Eldon for not being like her, for not mentoring more associates and taking more of the workload. Eldon could feel the unspoken animosity building up between him and his boss. He began to isolate himself. A year passed with nothing resolved.

An insightful managing partner called in the department head and told her that the junior professionals wanted to transfer out of her department. The partner explained that if she wanted to progress further, she would need to prioritize her career goals. The current track wasn't going to pay off long-term.

The managing partner assigned her a coach who taught the young star how to create and refine a focused, clearly communicated, personal agenda. For instance, the first item was to better leverage her time by reengaging with Eldon. The department head held a number of key meetings with Eldon where she realized that Eldon wasn't resentful because he didn't get chosen as department head. Instead, she recognized that her own resentment stemmed from Eldon's refusal to treat her like a partner. As they spent more time together, associates began to seek out Eldon to learn from him. Eldon started to show interest in learning how to sell. Over time, Eldon began to feel that he mattered, that someone besides himself cared about his career. The reconnection process had started. The department head had saved a valuable resource for the firm.

Occasions for Disconnection

There are many points at which young professionals feel disconnected and want to leave a firm. It's essential to be aware of these critical junctures so that leaders at all levels can make the appropriate interventions to keep associates connected. Too many young professionals are leaving at the wrong times for the wrong reasons.

Unrealized Expectations

Many associates leave their first employment contract because their expectations are not met. More specifically, they believe firms fail to keep recruiting promises or help them adjust to their new environments. Some of their expectations may be unrealistic, yet associates want firms to be realistic. As one new associate observed,

> I joined the company hoping my perceptions and expectations would match. I soon realized the recruiting process was disconnected from reality once I joined the firm. The recruiting team told me what I wanted to hear. I listened for what I wanted to hear. Promises were made, but reality has set in. When I didn't get the assignment I wanted in the media group, it felt as if the firm didn't know what to do with me. It quickly became apparent that my immediate boss had limited management experience and wasn't interested in the process of management. He was fighting his own organizational battles. I was surprised how quickly I began to think about leaving the firm. I knew I needed to do something to change the situation, but I wasn't sure what to do or where to turn. I felt like if I talked to anyone about my concerns I would be seen as weak. And I learned in business school to keep my head down, work very hard, learn the business, and have a great attitude.

The challenge is to be aspirational yet realistic with professionals. We have seen good leaders balance this tension by simply showing interest and paying attention at the right time.

The Transition from Expert to Producer-Manager

A second catalyst for disconnection often occurs as professionals move from doing the work itself and managing others. Most young professionals feel both internal desire and external pressure to begin managing in addition to doing the work. In most PSFs, ongoing pressure exists to focus on managing client expectations and managing professionals simultaneously; this pressure intensifies the higher one goes in a firm's hierarchy.

While these competing demands exist at all levels, professionals transitioning to managerial roles find it especially challenging. They must learn how to contribute through others and not just through their own individual contributions. As a result, delegation is a key skill for them to master as we discussed earlier, in chapter 7. Some professionals, though, find delegating a challenge, given how much satisfaction they derive from doing the actual job. They also must learn to forgo short-term results by focusing on clients and strive to achieve more ambiguous successes by targeting long-term financial goals.

During this stage, firm leaders and those transitioning to managerial positions must develop a wider business perspective and help others to understand the broader business context and needs. The new producer-manager begins contributing to the performance of others through mentoring, facilitating ideas, and in other ways. This professional becomes competent at representing the work group on important issues and begins to build a strong internal network. As a result of these new responsibilities, the professional faces increased external and internal pressure. Clients may want the professional's time. Yet younger professionals require coaching and feedback. The demands pile up. If they receive little or no help in areas where they are struggling and begin viewing themselves as alone and isolated, the professionals feel disconnected.

Most top-tier, high-performing PSFs—Morgan Stanley is an example—are encouraging managers to put more focus on subordinates. In many regions, managing directors sponsor leadership seminars for young officers who must take on more project management, mentor junior professionals, and bring revenues to the bottom line. These learning and development seminars do more than teach content. Connecting across the firm with other professionals from other regions is as important as absorbing content. The give-and-take between managers from different regions creates a mosaic of problem-solving processes that fosters global connections.

The performance evaluation process, too, is often used to solidify connection with the firm during this phase of a professional's career. Senior professionals spend time in individual career development discussions with those employees moving from one career stage to another. They concentrate on career ambitions, organizational and individual goal alignment, individual capabilities, and long-term career interests.

The Paradox of "Arriving"

Surprisingly, another point at which professionals may feel a sense of disconnection is when they attain a long-sought career goal. When professionals "arrive" in their careers as a senior producer-manager or a partner, they often feel exhilarated, in the short-term. It is the same rush that most professionals experience when they attain a capstone position. At the same time, however, many people also report paradoxical feelings of emptiness. Some partners in PSFs acknowledge feeling adrift and ambitionless at this point in their careers. Some new partners ask themselves or others: "Is this it? Is this all there is?" Or, "Do I have to keep doing the same thing for the next fifteen years?"

Firms should recognize these signs as intervention points. They must reach out and extend the boundary of inclusion when employees reach a senior-level position—preferably within a few months. This is when the professional can contribute the most to the organization because of institutional knowledge, content knowledge, and established relationships within and outside the organization. Veteran professionals who leave represent a great loss to the system, so firms must intervene to prevent hasty departures.

The empty feeling of being adrift at this career stage can often be caused by accumulated fatigue and stress. Managers who have not paced themselves have little energy left once they are promoted to a senior level. Sabbaticals can reconnect partners to the fabric of the firm. This does not mean just taking time off, but using the time productively to recharge one's batteries and renew one's excitement about the firm and its work. In universities, faculty often teach at other schools or attend conferences to renew their creative juices and to engage in self-reflection. More and more, senior professionals are seeking education programs that give them a respite from the daily grind and an opportunity to acquire fresh knowledge and perspectives that they are eager to use when they return to the workplace.

When professionals become partners, they often realize that their workloads haven't changed. In fact, they have more responsibilities and more pressures. Unless the firm creates structured activities and processes for discussing these issues, malaise can set in for the professional.

Keeping Professionals Intellectually and Emotionally Engaged

Certainly firms cannot maintain strong, ongoing relationships with all professionals. Some people do burn out because of their particular personalities. Some leave to pursue great opportunities and would depart no matter what a firm did. No doubt, some professionals should move on because they do not fit with the firm, cannot meet the firm's expectations, or realize that their skills are better suited elsewhere.

Others, though, leave prematurely or at the worst possible times. They may also remain physically but are so burned out or alienated that they contribute far less than they could under different circumstances. To prevent or remedy these problems and keep people connected, consider the following actions, all of which flow from the integrated leadership model:

- Articulate the direction and strategy of the project.

- Communicate expectations and provide resources for meeting them.

- Ask professionals to be accountable after they have executed a project.

- Remember that small acknowledgments and recognitions count in small ways.

- Make time each week to recognize your professionals.

- Give choices.

Communicate Expectations and Provide Resources for Meeting Them

From the moment a professional joins a firm, he or she should understand how the organization measures success. This is an essential part of the direction and execution dimensions of the integrated firm. Bosses should make expectations clear and provide feedback when professionals are going off course. As part of this communication process, leaders should listen to professionals carefully and consistently. Feedback has a much greater impact when professionals feel their concerns have been taken seriously. They are more likely to respond to expectations and feel included rather than excluded when their questions and complaints are taken seriously.

Organizations must take ownership of the socialization or induction process. They should provide competent mentors and promote dynamic networking through processes consistent with its culture and structure. Firms must also make learning and coaching available through professionally staffed development centers that match individual and organizational needs. Learning and development programs can inculcate the values of an organization and teach concepts, share information, and prepare employees for assignments and roles. Lateral-hire programs, new employee programs, management and leadership training, and technical training either communicate or equip professionals to satisfy an organization's expectations.

As we have discussed, performance management can be a highly effective means of managing expectations with respect to professional development and change. By holding managers accountable for regular, honest conversations with their professionals, expectations are managed in real time. The give-and-take that characterizes this feedback helps professionals feel valued and offers direction to make them become even more valuable.

Integrated leaders take all these actions within a framework of setting direction, building commitment, ensuring execution, and providing a personal example. In other words, they see communicating expectations as a key leadership responsibility, one that helps them let everyone know the direction of the firm and each person's role. By their personal example as well as policy, firm leaders communicate expectations and provide resources to meet them. They put their weight behind learning and development programs, for instance, demonstrating to everyone that these programs are important to helping professionals meet the firm's expectations.

Express Respect

Firms that want professionals with courage and high aspirations bear some responsibility for cultivating these traits. As we showed in chapter 2, Infosys Technologies chairman Narayana Murthy maintains that organizations need to be able to get their people to believe they can walk on water.[7] Great leaders communicate their faith that people can achieve more than they thought through one-on-one talks. Building up people's confidence in this way frequently translates into a strengthened commitment to the firm. Professionals begin to see the organization as a cause. Some create and others readily join internal communities that embrace organizational values and philosophies. Confident professionals connect more easily to the organization's core, as the following example illustrates.

An executive of a midwestern money management firm believed that he could gather helpful information from employees who were not yet part of the system. He assumed that these individuals would be truthful, since they had not been conditioned to tell the boss what he wanted to hear. After interviewing all professionals who had been with the firm for three months, the executive not only found what he was looking for, he also received a bonus. The new professionals felt honored and special because the executive took the time to solicit their opinions about how the organization could be improved. Moreover, the associates developed a deeper commitment to the organization's values and goals, because the executive communicated his intent by valuing their opinions.

Similarly, global investment bank Goldman Sachs has designated a practice partner who is charged with the care and feeding of other partners. This partner travels extensively throughout the firm conducting detailed career development discussions. Because the practice partner is highly accomplished as a banker, and because senior management takes the position seriously, other partners perceive the importance of the role. When the practice partner talks, people listen. Moreover, they solicit his advice on everything from human capital decisions to human capital strategies. This role helps Goldman Sachs communicate the importance it attaches to professionals' career development, and the practice partner's mandate is a constant reminder to all firm members of this priority.

Again, this is integrated leadership in action. The practice partner sets an example that resonates throughout the firm, going above and beyond the traditional PSF leadership model. By establishing a practice partner position or similar role, firms send the implicit message that they are not just concerned with the bottom line and "what can you do for me now." Accenture Consulting, for instance, has assigned responsibility for all new hires in a particular office to a "class dean." Acting in the capacity of adviser, confidant, or housemaster, the dean ensures that each new hire has at least one meaningful assignment, a mentor, and the resources needed to succeed in building a network within the organization. The dean assesses whether new professionals understand the purpose of the firm and of their work in the context of the organization's goals. The dean's overarching goal is to ensure that professionals are growing and developing, contributing to the firm's core mission, and staying connected. The dean's presence and assistance conveys how much the firm respects its professionals as individuals rather than as cogs in a machine.

Give the Gift of Time

Professionals at all levels want senior partners to be interested in what they are doing, interested in how they are spending their time, and interested in them. They want equal time with senior partners. Even when they think they're fairly allocating their time, senior partners often don't realize that they are spending many more hours with some people than others.

The division head at a consulting firm learned that certain direct reports were feeling alienated and frustrated that other members were receiving all his attention. Discovering that he had no idea to whom he was allocating his time, the division head began tracking the frequency of his interactions with his direct reports. He quickly realized that he was neglecting certain solid performers. Further, he discovered that some of his most loyal performers never checked in but were out seeing clients. He adjusted his schedule and made time for every direct report, not just those who made noise or demanded attention. Though it was impossible to measure whether he improved levels of connectedness in his group, he did not lose a single person to another firm in the following year, and he noticed a marked improvement of job satisfaction and enthusiasm in 360-degree feedback. (See chapter 8 for an example of another leader who used this approach).

Make Time Each Week to Recognize Your Professionals

Although this may seem like a small thing, written acknowledgment provides tangible evidence that a professional exists and is seen as an individual. The managing director of a large consulting firm makes a point of sending handwritten notes to professionals who he believes are doing a great job but have received few accolades. A recipient of one of the notes said that he had kept it for over a year because of the pride and encouragement he received from it. Although gestures such as these are extremely important, professionals do not need coddling or flattering; what they need is recognition of their real contributions. They will be grateful for praise.

Give Choices

Many PSFs lack systematic, creative ways to retain professionals. Typically, they ignore frustrated professionals until they walk out or give up. What firms should be doing is identifying developmental needs and finding ways to meet those needs. Of course, it is not always possible to give professionals the biggest and best assignments if they are not ready for them. Nor is it possible to provide every professional with the desired salary and bonus. On the other hand, firms have a range of resources at their disposal for meeting a professional's need for recognition and respect. From sending a professional offsite to a prestigious development program to making him or her a member of a special, industrywide team, to allowing an individual the chance to pursue a pet project, firms can offer alternatives—alternatives attuned the professional's particular interests and concerns. We emphasize that this must not be a haphazard process. The challenge is to create a system that offers professionals options and gives them a certain amount of freedom to blaze their own paths in order to facilitate feelings of connection.

The Constant Battle Against Disconnection

Some leaders of PSFs recognize the need to foster connectivity within the firm. John Mack, chairman of Morgan Stanley, is well-known for creating cultures that focus on teamwork, collaboration, and high expectations, as the following quote illustrates:

> I have met with junior people in lunches, dinners, and in small groups throughout my career. I've got to teach my senior managers that they have to reach out and pay attention to their professionals. Managers must focus on more than short-term profits . . . It has been an ongoing challenge to get managers to focus on managing their people for the long-term. The last thing they want to do is spend another evening away from home being with their subordinates.[8]

Like Mack, other PSF leaders are realizing that when professionals feel excluded and isolated, the firm has a major problem.

When professionals are left out, they are not focusing on their careers. Instead, they are concerned with survival, career doubts, and figuring how to get back into the club—the club being defined as anything from a small work group to a large division.

The integrated leaders who are adept at forging this connection are especially valuable in PSFs, where stress levels are high and job changing is frequent. Their ability to communicate with professionals and convince them that the firm cares about their careers and job satisfaction is a competency that can translate into competitive advantage. In global firms, in matrix organizations, and in firms that have highly trained knowledge workers, the need for connecting leaders is becoming more apparent. Just being a member of a firm today does not insure security, automatic growth, and development. All professionals go through stages of feeling undervalued and underappreciated, especially when bosses leave, client shifts occur, and other changes cause them to wonder about their place in the firm.

Working in organizations can be a very stressful and lonely endeavor. Connectors create a safety net to catch those professionals who may be ready to leave the system or who are not engaged in the enterprise. The dilemma for most PSFs is that they do not explicitly value or reward those professionals who spend the time and effort focused on the human side of the enterprise. Great PSFs need to confront this deficiency. The time has come to value the professionals who keep the culture dynamic and supportive through their ability to connect people throughout the firm.

Notes

Introduction

1. David H. Maister, *Managing the Professional Service Firm* (New York: Free Press, 1993), chapter 2.

Chapter 1

1. David H. Maister, *Managing the Professional Service Firm* (New York: Free Press, 1993); and Jay W. Lorsch and Peter Mathias, "When Professionals Have to Manage," *Harvard Business Review*, July–August 1987.

2. Maister, *Managing the Professional Service Firm*.

3. Maister emphasizes in his book why leaders went into the profession, e.g., to become technical experts and problem solvers.

Chapter 2

1. William F. Joyce, Nitin Nohria, and Bruce Roberson, *What Really Works: The 4+2 Formula for Sustained Business Success* (New York: Harper Collins, 2003).

2. Chris Argyris, *Strategy, Change and Defensive Reactions* (Boston: Pitman, 1985), chapter 2.

3. M. Diane Burton, "Rob Parson at Morgan Stanley (A)," Case 498-054 (Boston: Harvard Business School, 1998).

4. Robert Eccles and Dwight Crane, *Doing Deals: Investment Banks at Work* (Boston: Harvard Business School Press, 1988), chapter 1.

5. Max De Pree, *Leadership Is an Art* (New York: Doubleday, 1989).

6. Jim Collins, *Good to Great: Why Some Companies Make the Leap and Others Don't* (New York: HarperBusiness, 2001).

Chapter 3

1. Alfred Chandler, *The Visible Hand* (Cambridge: Belknap Press of Harvard University Press, 1977).

2. John J. Gabarro, "Prologue: The Emerging Modern Law Firm, Corporate Model vs. Stratified Apprenticeship," in *Managing the Modern Law Firm*, ed. Laura Empson (Oxford: Oxford University Press, 2007).

3. Karl Weick, *The Social Psychology of Organizing* (New York: McGraw Hill, 1979).

4. Jay Lorsch and Peter Mathias, "When Professionals Have to Manage," *Harvard Business Review,* July–August 1987.

5. Gabarro, "Prologue: The Emerging Modern Law Firm." A sense of historical context is given in Elliot A. Krause, *Death of the Guilds* (New Haven, CT: Yale University Press, 1996), 1–29.

6. Michael L. Tushman and Charles A. O'Reilly, *Winning Through Innovation: A Practical Guide to Leading Organizational Change and Renewal* (Boston: Harvard Business School Press, 1997).

7. Interview, May 2004, with CEO who prefers to remain anonymous.

Chapter 4

1. Thomas DeLong and Ashish Nanda, *Professional Services: Text and Cases* (Boston: McGraw-Hill Irwin, 2003).

2. David H. Maister, *Managing the Professional Service Firm* (New York: Free Press, 1993).

3. Morton Hansen, Nitin Nohria, and Thomas Tierney, "What's Your Strategy for Managing Knowledge?" *Harvard Business Review*, March–April 1999, 106–116.

4. We do not consider outsourcing to be a professional service but rather a related service; therefore it is not included on the continuum.

Chapter 5

1. David H. Maister, *Managing the Professional Service Firm* (New York: Free Press, 1993). Also see David H. Maister, "Balancing the Professional Service Firm," *Sloan Management Review* 24, no. 1 (1982): 15–29.

2. Maister, *Managing the Professional Service Firm.*

3. Ibid., 21–30.

4. Ibid.

5. Ibid., 30.

6. Stephen R. Covey, *The Seven Habits of Highly Effective People: Restoring the Character Ethic* (New York: Simon & Schuster, 1989).

7. Thomas DeLong and Vineeta Vijayaraghavan, "Harrah's Entertainment, Inc: Rewarding Our People," Case 403-008 (Boston: Harvard Business School, 2002).

8. Maister, *Managing Professional Service Firms.*

Chapter 6

1. Jay W. Lorsch and Thomas J. Tierney, *Aligning the Stars* (Boston: Harvard Business School Press, 2002), 10–11.

2. Adrian Wooldridge, "A Survey of Talent," *The Economist*, October 7, 2006, 5.

3. Intellinex LLC was acquired by Affiliated Computer Services, Inc. (ACS) in 2006.

4. P. Lawrence and J. Lorsch, "Differentiation and Integration in Complex Organizations," *Administrative Science Quarterly* 12 (1967): 1–30.

Chapter 7

1. David C. McClelland, *Human Motivation* (Glenview, IL: Scott Foresman, 1983). See also David C. McClelland, *Power: The Inner Experience* (New York: Irvington, 1975).

2. Ibid.

3. Social motive theory has been eclipsed by the Five Factor Theory (Responsibility, Openness, Hostility, Extraversion, and Neuroticism) as predictive dimensions of personality, because the factors (Big Five) identify more fundamental traits of personality. See Robert McCrea and Paul Costa, *Personality in Adulthood: A Five-factor Theory Perspective* (New York: Guildford, 2003). In our experience, however, the five factors are not as effective in predicting the motivation to perform at work, and except for the responsibility trait, none of them singly is as characteristic of professionals as the need for achievement.

4. David C. McClelland, *The Achievement Motive* (New York: Irvington, 1976), 82. Also see Bonner Ritchie and P. H. Thompson, eds., *Organizations and People* (Boston: West, 1976).

Chapter 8

1. Thomas DeLong and Vineeta Vijayaraghavan, "Let's Hear It for B Players," *Harvard Business Review,* June 2003, 96–102.

2. Lotte Bailyn, *Breaking the Mold: Women, Men, and Time in the New Corporate World* (New York: Free Press, 1993).

Chapter 9

1. Peter F. Drucker, "The New Society of Organizations," *Harvard Business Review*, September–October 1992, 100.

2. Frederick Reichheld, *The Loyalty Effect* (Boston: Harvard Business School Press, 1996), 95.

3. Harvard Business School Career Services, internal documents.

4. Reichheld, *The Loyalty Effect*, 94.

5. Ibid., 103. Factoring in the average attrition rate, the real investment needed to produce a profitable broker is considerably more than the $100,000 noted by Reichheld. The firm will actually have to hire and train three new brokers to get one who survives long enough to make an acceptable return. So the true investment in each long-term broker asset is closer to $300,000. This helps explain why an increase in broker retention from 80 percent to 90 percent will improve the value of the average new broker by 155 percent.

6. Edgar H. Schein, *Career Anchors: Discovering Your Real Values* (San Diego, CA: Jossey-Bass/Pfeiffer, 1990).

7. Narayana Murthy, lecture at Harvard Business School, April 20, 2001.

8. Authors' interview with John Mack, December 1996.

Index

academia, 14, 200
Accenture Consulting, 5, 65, 80, 83,
    94, 106, 116–117, 204
accounting. *See* public accounting
achievement orientation. *See* high-
    need-for-achievement personality
acquisitions
    failure of mergers, 9–10
    mergers and acquisitions markets,
        159
    by product-producing firms, as
        leadership challenge, 9–10
ACS (Intellinex), 130
action plans, 157
action-research model, 111
actuarial services, 57
    codified body of knowledge in, 45
    practice segmentation in, 103
    pressures of commoditization in,
        99
actuarial software, 45, 71
advertising, 14, 148
advisory services
    migrating to, 84–85
    tax advisory services, 45, 99, 103
affiliation needs, 149, 165

alienation. *See also* connection;
    disconnection
    avoiding, communication and, 103
    personal interactions with partners
        and, 180–181
alignment of internal structures,
    141–146
    case history: Herbert Smith,
        135–141
    in direction setting, 142–143
    in execution, 144–145
    in gaining commitment, 143–144
    in personal example, 145–146
    strategic differentiation and, 125
alignment of practice
    with associate expectations, 96
    with client needs, 94–95
    with competitive markets, 4
    with segment needs, 89
    with strategic positioning, 141
alternatives, provision of, 205–206
ambidextrous organizations, 64–65, 67
American Management Association,
    190
A players. *See* "star" performers,
    demanding nature of

About the Authors

Thomas J. DeLong is the Philip J. Stomberg Professor of Management Practice in the organizational behavior area at the Harvard Business School. Before joining the Harvard faculty, DeLong was chief development officer and managing director of Morgan Stanley Group, Inc., where he was responsible for the firm's human capital and focused on issues of organizational strategy regarding people, organizational change, and globalization. DeLong coauthored the *Harvard Business Review* articles "Managing Talent: The Key Challenge for Today's Professional Service Firm" and "Let's Hear It for B Players" as well as the book *Professional Services: Cases and Texts* (McGraw-Hill/Irwin 2003).

John J. Gabarro is Baker Foundation Professor at the Harvard Business School. Gabarro is the author or coauthor of eight books including *Breaking Through* with David Thomas, which won the 2001 George Terry Prize, given by the Academy of Management for outstanding contribution to management theory and practice. He also wrote *The Dynamics of Taking Charge,* which won the New Perspectives in Leadership Award and was named one of the best business books of the year by the *Wall Street Journal*. Gabarro is also a recipient of the McKinsey Foundation Prize and the Johnson Smith Knisely Foundation Award for research on executive leadership.

Robert J. Lees is a consultant to leaders of professional service firms. Lees has had an extensive career in PSFs, having most recently served as director of professional development at Morgan Stanley. Previously, he served as director of professional development for Ernst & Young's U.K. firm, then as Ernst & Young's global head of human resources, and subsequently director of Ernst & Young's Global Leadership Center in Cambridge, Massachusetts. Lees is coauthor of the HBR article "Managing Talent: The Key Challenge for Today's Professional Service Firm."